CHICKEN SOUP FOR THE TEA LOVER'S SOUL

CHICKEN SOUP FOR THE TEA LOVER'S SOUL

Stories Steeped in Comfort

Jack Canfield
Mark Victor Hansen
Patricia Lorenz

Health Communications, Inc.
Deerfield Beach, Florida

www.hcibooks.com
www.chickensoup.com

We would like to acknowledge the many publishers and individuals who granted us permission to reprint the cited material. Any content not specifically attributed to an author was written by Patricia Lorenz. The stories that were penned anonymously, that are in the public domain, or that were written by Jack Canfield, Mark Victor Hansen, or Patricia Lorenz are not included in this listing.

My Best Cup of Tea. Reprinted by permission of Shirley Babcock. ©2006 Shirley Babcock.

Sweet Dreams. Reprinted by permission of B. J. Taylor. ©2007 B. J. Taylor.

Biscuits and Tea. Reprinted by permission of Susan Engebrecht. ©2007 Susan Engebrecht.

Tea-Room Follies. Reprinted by permission of Sherrie Eldridge. ©2006 Sherrie Eldridge.

Steeped in Cherished Memories. Reprinted by permission of Eileen Valinoti. ©2007 Eileen Valinoti.

(Continued on page 228)

Library of Congress Cataloging-in-Publication Data

Chicken soup for the tea lover's soul : stories steeped in comfort /
    [compiled by] Jack Canfield, Mark Victor Hansen, Patricia Lorenz.
        p. cm.
    ISBN-13: 978-0-7573-0624-2 (trade paper)
    ISBN-10: 0-7573-0624-1 (trade paper)
    1. Tea. 2. Tea—Anecdotes. I. Canfield, Jack, 1944- II. Hansen,
Mark Victor. III. Lorenz, Patricia.
    TX817.T3C38 2007
    394.1'2—dc22

                                                                    2007025774

Publisher: Health Communications, Inc.
3201 S.W. 15th Street
Deerfield Beach, FL 33442–8190

Cover design by Larissa Hise Henoch
Inside book formatting by Theresa Peluso and Lawna Patterson Oldfield

We dedicate this book
to the tea drinkers of the world,
who find such splendid comfort in tea,
the world's most popular beverage.

Contents

1. DELECTABLE DELIGHTS

Acknowledgments

Compiling, editing, and publishing a book requires the energy and expertise of many people. First, a huge thank-you to our families. Jack's wife, Inga, and their children, Christopher, Travis, Riley, Oran, and Kyle, for all their love and support. Mark's family, Patty, Elisabeth, and Melanie, for once again sharing and lovingly supporting us in creating yet another book.

Patricia enjoys the love and support of her family: her parents, Ed and Bev Kobbeman; her four children, Jeanne, Julia, Michael and Andrew, and their spouses; her eight grandchildren, Hailey, Hannah, Zachary, Casey, Riley, Chloe, Adeline, and Ethan; her brother and sister and their families; and her many friends scattered around the country.

The vision and commitment of our publisher, Peter Vegso, brings Chicken Soup for the Soul to the world.

Patty Aubery and Russ Kalmaski share this journey with love, laughter, and endless creativity. Patty Hansen has handled the legal and licensing aspects of each book thoroughly and competently, and Laurie Hartman has been a precious guardian of the Chicken Soup for the Soul brand. Michelle Adams, Noelle Champagne, D'ette Corona, Lauren Edelstein, Jody Emme, Teresa Esparza, Jesse Ianniello, Tanya Jones, Debbie Lefever, Barbara

LoMonaco, Mary McKay, Dee Dee Romanello, Gina Romanello, Veronica Romero, Brittany Shaw, Shanna Vieyra, Lisa Williams, and Robin Yerian support Jack's and Mark's businesses with skill and love.

Thank you to Theresa Peluso, a fellow *Chicken Soup* coauthor, who assisted in putting this book together, kept us organized and on schedule, and made it easy. We appreciate Andrea Gold's, effort in editing this book and the work of HCI's editorial department, directed by Michelle Matriciani, and the HCI creative team, led by Larissa Hise Henoch, whose efforts make each book special. And to the rest of the staff at HCI, who for their sheer numbers must go nameless, who get all of our books into readers' hands, copy after copy, with dedication and professionalism.

Readers around the world enjoy *Chicken Soup for the Soul* in more than thirty-six languages because of the efforts of Claude Choquette and Luc Jutras at Montreal Contacts, The Rights Agency.

Our thanks and appreciation go out to the hundreds of writers who opened their hearts and submitted such delectable stories about their enjoyment of tea. We regret that we couldn't publish them all in this book.

And we wish to acknowledge the volunteers who graciously donated time to help us select these stories. Thank you: Katherine Bontrager, Jennifer Campbell, Deb Karpek, Katy McManus-Semphill, Julie Miller, Marsha Oldfield, Melanie Rigney, Sallie Rodman, Diane Smith, Ken Thompson, Patty Tinsdale, Maddy Underbrock, Dave Wilkins, Dona Williams, Heather Young, Phyllis Zeno, and Lora Zill.

Introduction

When I was very young, possibly in the early grade-school years, my mother and father, Ed and Lucy Kobbeman, invited me to sit with them in the evenings at the old walnut kitchen table in our home in Rock Falls, Illinois. Mother would boil water, dip a tea bag in my cup for just twenty or thirty seconds, then add it to her cup for a full brewing. Mom, Dad, and I would sit there and talk about life, school, family events. It made me feel so very grown-up to not only be included in their talks, but to be allowed to drink tea with them. I think I actually enjoyed the tea even more than the cookies that sometimes accompanied our little tea party.

Those sweet evenings were the beginning of a lifetime of delicious tea drinking for me, and to this day I have never had a cup of coffee in my life. My beverage of choice during my entire adult life has been tea, glorious tea. These days I have eighty different flavors of tea from many countries sitting in glass jars that I have hand-painted on my kitchen counter. I learned years ago that tea must be kept sealed in a tight, glass container or it loses its flavor.

I think I've enjoyed more cups of tea than anyone I know. I drink tea alone or with friends, family, neighbors, or anyone who stops by.

On my kitchen cabinet, right next to my stove where my white teakettle resides, is a quote I cherish from British Prime Minister William Gladstone:

> *If you're cold, tea will warm you.*
> *If you're heated, it will cool you.*
> *If you're depressed, it will cheer you.*
> *If you're excited, it will calm you.*

I believe those words, mainly because I've experienced them all. Somehow, a cup of tea in my favorite hand-crafted ocean-blue pottery mug with the large handle just makes life a better, warmer/cooler, happier, calmer, and more contented place to be than if I was slurping sodas out of a can or hoisting water bottles for every ounce of my prescribed daily liquids.

Tea is charming in its variety of flavors. It's civilized because it can't be hurried. It's universal. There isn't a country in the world where the people don't drink tea mingled with delightful, unique-to-that-country traditions.

Tea is refreshing. It gets you off to a good start in the morning, makes for a lovely midday break, and is the perfect nightcap before bed.

Universally celebrated in drama, poetry, commerce, and international relationships, tea has had an influence on lives all over the world. In England, drinking tea is a social custom. English afternoon tea combines the best cups of tea in dainty teacups with tea breads, finger sandwiches, sausage rolls, scones, and sponge and seed cakes. Soothing and civilized, the ritual of afternoon tea offers a welcome respite from the hustle and bustle of daily life as the tea drinkers enjoy pleasant conversation and determined relaxation.

In Japan, tea drinking has ceremonial overtones. China has cultivated and extolled tea for centuries. America found tea a favorite brew in colonial times and a political force during the Revolutionary War.

Sri Lanka, China, India, and Kenya are among the tropical and subtropical regions that produce tea, both the green and black variety.

The difference between black and green tea is simple. Black tea leaves are picked, allowed to wither and oxidize or ferment, and then are dried. Green teas are steamed and dried, but never fermented.

Part of the fun of being a tea drinker is the way tea drinking keeps you busy. First, you get to swish the bag around in the cup of hot water, adding lemon, sugar, milk, cream, honey, or any combination of the above. Then, when the tea is the right strength, you lift the bag out of the cup onto your teaspoon, gently wrapping the attached string under and over the top of the spoon and the wet bag so it can be squeezed with the string a couple of times. This keeps the bag from dripping all over the table when you dispose of it.

Then, when you're ready for another cup, you start all over, pouring, dangling, swishing, adding milk, cream, sweetener, or lemon . . . creating a masterpiece of flavor.

The beauty of tea is that it is never boring. There are hundreds, perhaps thousands, of flavors to choose from in all different combinations of black, green, or natural herb teas. For instance, a deliciously simple-tasting tea called

Country Peach Spice is actually a combination of hibiscus flowers, cinnamon, roasted chicory root, rosehips, hawthorn berries, blackberry leaves, orange peel, tilia flowers, peaches, natural peach flavors, nutmeg, and other natural flavors.

Next time you reach for the coffeepot, consider a hot cup of tea instead. It's a great way to break the caffeine habit since tea contains much less caffeine than coffee. And, of course, herbal teas contain no jitter-causing caffeine.

Goodness, look at the clock. It's tea time!

Patricia Lorenz

1

DELECTABLE DELIGHTS

The Last Great Tea Party

Taking tea together encourages an
atmosphere of intimacy when you slip off
the timepiece in your mind and cast your
fate to a delight of tasty tea, tiny foods,
and thoughtful conversation.

Gail Greco

A ndrew and I awoke to one of the coldest January
days ever recorded in Milwaukee. The actual
temperature was twenty-two degrees below zero,
with a wind-chill factor of seventy below. Most schools in
southeastern Wisconsin were closed because the risk of
frostbite was too great for children waiting for school
buses.

The furnace was running almost constantly, but the
house was still cold. I was wearing two pairs of pants, a
turtleneck, and a pullover sweater, and stood shivering in
the kitchen. Just then, Andrew, my almost-six-foot-tall
eighth-grader, walked in and asked in a perfect British
accent, "Say, Mum, don't you think it's 'bout time for a
spot of tea?"

I laughed as I grabbed the teakettle to fill it with water.
Andrew was in drama class that semester, and he was

fascinated with his Scotch, Irish, English, French, and German ancestry, especially the different accents of each language. I looked closely at my son, whose father had died five years earlier, and was filled with appreciation at what a warm and easy relationship Andrew and I had developed over the years.

"Why, certainly, my good man," I declared with as much drama as I could muster.

Andrew's eyes twinkled. He knew the scene was set. From that moment, we became English subjects. My British accent was muddled, but I tried to mimic the drama in Andrew's more perfected version. "Do you fancy a spot of Earl Grey or Jasmine? English or Irish Breakfast? What flavor grabs your fancy this brisk morning?" I asked.

"Say, Mum, what is the difference between high tea and low tea?"

"Well, lad, low tea, which is usually called afternoon tea, is generally served at a low coffee or end table while the guests relax on a sofa or parlor chairs. High tea is served at a high dining-room table in the early evening, our traditional supper hour. More substantial foods are served at high tea, you see." As a woman who had never had a cup of coffee in her life, but who loved tea, I was enjoying this opportunity to draw my son into my wonderful world of tea drinking.

Andrew rubbed his hands together as if warming them over an old English kitchen fireplace. "So, Mum, let's have low tea on the coffee table in the living room. I'll make the preparations while you put on the kettle."

Before I could remind my son that I had work to do in

my home office, Andrew cleared the low, round oak coffee table of magazines, grabbed a cotton lace runner in the dining room, and spread it across the table-half closest to the sofa. Then he retrieved a centerpiece of silk flowers from the marble-top chest in the hallway and placed it behind the lace runner. For the final touch, he moved our small, solid oak mantel clock to the coffee table. The clock's rhythmic ticking, which could now be heard in the kitchen, made it seem that we were actually living in a drafty old English manor outside London.

Next, Andrew opened the china cupboard and retrieved my small English blue and white teapot, two delicate, antique, hand-painted bone-china teacups and saucers, the silver cream-and-sugar set, and a silver tray.

"I do declare, Mum, I can't see my face in the silver. It's in dire need of a good polishing."

"I'll get right on it, Master Andrew," I said with a wink.

Andrew set the table with two sandwich plates trimmed with flowers and gold paint that he found behind the silver. Then, in the drawer, he searched for two perfect napkins, settling on dark green linen, with a large, hand-embroidered yellow maple leaf on each corner.

"Here, the tray is ready. Gleaming, don't you think?" I proclaimed proudly. He smiled as a glint of his true English heritage shone through his eyes, and his face was mirrored in the silver.

As we waited for the water to heat and I carefully arranged sandwiches on the shining silver tray, Andrew dashed off to his room where he scoured his childhood collection of 160 hats, hanging on all four walls, for a proper hat to wear to what was most certainly going to be a very proper low tea.

My handsome son emerged wearing a plaid tam my godparents had given him after a trip they took to Scotland and England. Andrew had also slipped into an old man's floppy green herringbone sport coat I'd picked up at Goodwill to wear in my workroom on cold days. I stood back and looked at my son. The hat and jacket had transformed his tall, trim body into a gentleman as striking as an English lord.

"Mum, don't you suppose you need a proper hat and skirt for the occasion?" He winked at me and shooed me off to my bedroom to change.

I headed for my own five-piece hat collection and emerged with a simple beige wide-brimmed straw hat with a single feather protruding off to the side. To my cranberry-colored sweater I attached an antique round pin with multi-colored stones that had belonged to Andrew's great-grandmother. A long black matronly skirt pulled on over my pants completed my outfit.

We were the perfect lord and lady. The teakettle whistled. As I poured the water into the proper teapot and added loose English Breakfast tea encased in a large chrome tea ball, Andrew tuned the radio to an FM station playing classical music. He offered me his arm as we entered the living room and made ourselves comfortable on the sofa.

By now, my character in our English play had evolved into a sort of beloved great-aunt who lived in a castle high on an English countryside and was absolutely delighted that her young nephew had dropped in for an unexpected visit. Suddenly, I wanted to know everything about this young man as I watched him carefully pour tea into the hardly-ever-used delicate teacups.

"So, tell me, Sir Andrew, what are your plans? Where are you going in this great adventure of life?"

Andrew leaned back on the throw pillows behind us as he sipped his tea and stroked his chin. "Well, it's a long road, you know. I still have four years of high school after this year, then college. Sometimes I wonder how I'll ever afford to attend college."

I reminded him that financial aid would be available just as it had been for his older sisters and brother. We talked about how he might get into one of his dream schools if he kept up his grades.

We slid into conversation about girls. Andrew looked out the floor-to-ceiling windows into the barren treetops and said slowly, "The girls. I think they all think I'm a geek."

"Oh, surely not! Why, Andrew, my good man, you're handsome, smart, funny. I bet the girls love you. You just don't know it yet."

Andrew sipped the steaming tea. Then he turned and said, "I don't fight much, so they probably say I'm a wimp."

My eyes rested on Andrew's size-thirteen feet, which proclaimed that his six-foot growth spurt was not over. I reassured him that not fighting was much more manly, something the high-school girls would certainly appreciate.

As time passed, we talked about music, sports, weather, God, and the school mixer coming up the next week. We watched a squirrel on the deck outside the windows eating corn off a cob. I felt myself opening up to the sensitive young man before me. I told Andrew how scared I was the year before, when I quit my regular job to start a business in my home. I told him I was lonely sometimes. He nodded, poured a tiny bit of skim milk into his tea, and picked up another tea sandwich. I took a deep breath and continued, "Someday, I'd love to meet a wonderful, interesting man with a great sense of humor and deep faith." I looked into the eyes of my son, pretending to be my nephew in drafty old England, and said, "I'd like to get married again someday, Andrew. I don't want to grow old alone."

The cold morning turned warm and wonderful as we each took turns talking and listening intently to what the other had to say. We both revealed parts of ourselves that had been neglected. Every so often, Andrew poured more tea for each of us. As he picked up the tiny sugar tongs, he'd ask, "One lump or two, Mum?" Then he'd politely offer the plate of tiny sandwiches.

On that cold winter day, when I was forty-eight and Andrew fourteen, we were transported into a world we both knew would only exist for that one morning. We would never again have a tea party like this one. Andrew would immerse himself in school, the basketball team, the junior-high band, his friends, the school play, the telephone, and video games at his best friend's house.

But it didn't matter because on that coldest day of the year, during those precious three hours as we stumbled through a mumbo jumbo of British phrases and inadequate but charming accents, my youngest child and I ate, drank, talked, shared, laughed, and warmed our souls to the very core. Andrew and I not only created a cherished memory, but we wrote and directed a play at the same instant we performed it. There was no audience, just Andrew and me, and cups of very good tea.

Patricia Lorenz

"One of the keys to happiness is letting it steep."

My Best Cup of Tea

A woman is like a tea bag:
you never know how strong she is
until she gets in hot water.

Nancy Reagan,
paraphrasing Eleanor Roosevelt

I worked for three years in the Republic of Botswana in southern Africa. Coming from the lush green forests and many lakes of northern Wisconsin, this land that was mostly Kalagadi Desert, with its vast expanse of tan sand, tan prickly thorn bushes, and gigantic tan termite hills, was at first sight startling in its sameness—except for the cloudless sky, which was brilliant blue. It was a period of drought. But it did not take me long before I saw and was enchanted by the beauty of the Kalagadi and its people.

The capital city, Gaborone, had a reservoir for water, making it like an oasis in the desert with its glorious scarlet jacaranda trees.

Botswana had been a protectorate of England until 1966 when the country gained independence peacefully. The English culture had a significant influence on the Botswana culture, the most enjoyable being tea drinking.

I was working with the Botswana Council for the Disabled under the Ministry of Health. When I wasn't working in the villages, which was most of the time, I occasionally attended the official meetings of Parliament in Gaborone. There was always a formal morning "tea break" when the government's business stopped, and tea was served to everyone. Then the cups were gathered up, and the pending business continued.

The cups of tea that were a true communion to my soul were those in the villages. On one trip with Nchele, the local health worker I traveled with, we rode through the Kalagadi Desert over illusive roads deeply rutted in fine sand, only stopping for a potty break behind a termite hill. We were on our way to a family who had been reported to us as needing our help. They had a three- or four-year-old little girl who only walked on her knees.

It was a very hot, dry, teeth-clacking jostle for three hours in a four-wheel-drive Jeep. Botswana had been suffering drought for three years. The sun and heat made mirages of silvery pools of water ahead of us on the desert sand. As we approached the family grounds, a scrawny goat nibbled on a stunted thorn bush, the only vegetation surviving the three-year drought. As we walked past the water barrel, we could see that it was nearly empty of the precious water the family had to carry from a very distant standpipe. As we neared the family's "yard," which was bordered by a foot-high enclosure made of packed mud and manure, we called out "koko," the polite way of announcing one's self. The father called out "tsena" (enter). A cloud of dust enveloped us as the children began to dance around us, squealing in joy.

As soon as the mother saw us coming, she went to the water barrel and scooped out a small amount of precious water with a battered pan already blackened from ages in the fire. As the water heated, she put in a handful of bush tea leaves. We sat on goat skins placed on the packed sand, and the tea was poured into a large tin cup, then offered to me. The mother offered it with her whole heart and a smile as brilliant as the blazing, hot sun, as though the water barrel had been full. As we all shared that one cup of tea, I knew there would never be a better-tasting cup of tea in all the world.

Shirley J. Babcock

Sweet Dreams

Tea is a meal for all seasons;
it's also suitable for all occasions.

Angela Hynes

"Why does he always have big projects on a Friday afternoon?" I wailed when I walked in the door after work.

"What's the matter, dear?" my mother-in-law said from the kitchen.

I threw my purse onto the counter. "Oh, my boss. He had me work late again. I didn't get out of the office until six o'clock. Now here it is almost seven. Why does he do that before the weekend?" I walked over to the refrigerator and opened it.

"Don't worry about dinner. I made lasagna," she said.

"Oh, that was nice of you. Let's chop up a salad to go with it." I pulled out the lettuce, cucumber, and tomatoes. We shared a cutting board, and chopped and sliced together, filling our bowls.

The lasagna came out of the oven hot and bubbly. It was delicious, but my mind swirled with thoughts of all the work waiting for me on my desk Monday morning. I was still miffed at my boss. We rinsed off the dinner dishes and put them into the dishwasher. My husband was on a three-day business trip, and this was the first night of my mother-in-law's visit. She'd be spending a few weeks with us before returning home.

"I'm sorry I came home in such a crabby mood. I didn't mean to take it out on you," I said.

"Don't worry about me. I can handle it. It's you I worry about. You shouldn't get so upset over work."

"I can't help it. My boss drives me crazy!"

"There were bosses like that in my day, too. There's only one way to deal with them," she said.

I was all ears, ready to hear the words of wisdom on how to put my boss in his place, how to tell him not to give me an overabundance of work, how to make him appreciate all that I do for him. "What's the secret?" I asked.

"A cup of tea."

"Tea? How can that help?"

"Let me show you. Sit down here on the sofa," she said as she patted the end.

I did as she directed. I sank into the soft pillow back and kicked off my shoes.

"Now close your eyes and relax. I'll be back in a few minutes."

I could hear her footsteps on the tile and knew she was in the kitchen. I listened as the cupboard door creaked when she took out some cups. The water ran in the sink. Then I heard the *ping-ping-ping* of the burner lighting on the gas stove. Minutes later, the kettle whistled.

"Okay, open your eyes," she said.

She stood in front of me with two steaming mugs. Dangling from the side of each was a string with a square piece of paper at the end.

"Here," she said as she handed me one of the mugs.

I took it with both hands. It wasn't too hot, just nice and warm. "Thanks," I said.

"Don't thank me yet. Sit and enjoy."

She joined me on the sofa, and we sat with our cups in our hands. I took a sip. It was good. "What kind is this?" I asked.

"It's a favorite of mine. I bring it with me wherever I go."

I felt myself relax as I sipped the tea, warmth flooding through not just my fingers and hands, but through my whole being. I felt calmer.

"So this tea—it makes bosses go away?" I asked, smiling.

She laughed. "No, nothing will do that. But it will make you forget about it for a little while."

We sat, drank, and enjoyed each other's company. We talked about some of the things we wanted to do while she was visiting. Time flew by. Soon, we were both down to the last drops in our cups. I got up and took the mugs to the kitchen sink.

"That was really good," I said, then covered my mouth as I yawned. "I'm ready to put on my pajamas and go to bed."

"Me, too," she replied.

"How about tomorrow night we watch a movie after dinner?" I said.

"Sounds great. I'll even make you another cup of tea."

She began climbing the stairs to the guest room. "Good night. See you in the morning."

"By the way, what was the name of that tea?" I asked.

She stopped halfway up the steps, turned her head toward me, and smiled. "Sweet Dreams," she said.

B. J. Taylor

Biscuits and Tea

Tea to the English is really
a picnic indoors.

Alice Walker, The Color Purple

T he legendary hostess, Gillian, and her husband
were coming to visit. I wanted their stay to be as
perfect as the one my husband had experienced at
their home the previous year.

My house underwent a scrubbing the likes of which it
seldom endured. The week's menu was plotted and
printed out, recipes included. All the shopping for ingre-
dients was complete. Crystal sparkled, and china plates
nestled in silver chargers that set off their delicate design.
They all stood waiting to serve us in elegant style.

At last, the time to relax was upon me. The knowledge
that fluffy blue towels tied with an ivory bow awaited
our guests filled me with a smug satisfaction. It would
have been nice to know how to fold towels into little
swans like they did in that fancy Mexican hotel, but my
ivory bow looked lovely. The welcome note leaned
against the lavender soap and a vase of forget-me-nots
on the sink was a most thoughtful touch. I'd done well,
and I knew it.

Muscles grew limp as my head drifted until it rested against the back of the La-Z-Boy. Silence settled around me. All was ready. Peace reigned. Suddenly, anxiety rumbled.

"Tea!" I shouted. "I forgot to buy tea."

My husband, that knight in faded blue jeans, charged into the room. "What?"

"Tea. I said TEA. Gillian must have tea. I only have herbal teas. The English don't drink that, do they? Oh, dear me, I don't know what she drinks." By this time I was out of the chair and flapping my arms in frustration.

My knight folded me into his arms, then gently sat us both on the sofa. "She'll bring her own tea."

Hope, like a delicate flower, began to blossom. "Do you really think so?"

"Yes, dear."

He was right. Gillian came bearing not only her own tea, but an insulated pot as well. All I needed to supply was a teakettle to warm water and cups to hold the elixir once it was brewed. I'm used to sloshing hot water over a tea bag, using the string to jiggle it up and down, splashing some 1% milk in, then calling it good. It's the American Way. But the English, now that's a different kettle altogether. Tea is a serious matter.

Gillian had a procedure, bordering on an art form, for making tea. It was difficult giving up being the perfect hostess and letting her loose in the kitchen to perform her magic. She was very much at home in the kitchen, singing as she rattled about. Her voice called out, "Missus? You will join me, won't you, darling?"

"Yes, that would be lovely." There was security in the fact that I'd done my part by setting out cups, dessert plates, and napkins—the linen ones, of course. Gillian entered the dining room with a teapot in one hand and a tin of homemade biscuits in the other.

Though our visits have become more frequent over the years, too many miles still separate us. Now the excitement over being together has nothing to do with menus, folding towels, or polishing silver. Gillian and I have become sisters. "Sisters by choice" is what we call this knitting together over biscuits and tea.

Susan Engebrecht

The Four Basic Teas

All four types of teas are derived from one single plant, the *Camellia sinensis*.

 Black and oolong teas are processed using oxygen (oxidation). When tea leaves are oxidized, they change in color and flavor. Black tea is the strongest brew because it is oxidized the longest.

 Green tea is not oxidized or fermented at all, which gives it a delicate, pungent flavor. Green tea leaves are steamed, rolled, then dried.

 Oolong tea is made from partially fermented leaves, which gives it a flavor somewhere between black and green tea.

 White tea is more rare than black, green, or oolong, and is thus more expensive. White tea, made from the same plant as the others, is simply made from leaves that are harvested before they're fully open. It has a light, sweet flavor.

Tea-Room Follies

There is always a great deal of poetry and
fine sentiment in a chest of tea.

Daniel Johns

T he tea room was so charming that I could hardly
wait to treat our daughters, Lisa and Chrissie,
both married and with children of their own. We'd
decided to take a week's vacation together in Florida, and
this was a rare opportunity for a mother/daughter date,
away from husbands, kids, and the daily pressures, to
make a cherished memory.

Outside the tea room was a life-sized, old-lady doll
seated in an antique wicker chair. She was dressed to the
nines—furs, pearls, fancy hat, and bright red lipstick
adorning her wrinkly smile.

As we were ushered to a little table in the corner, we
were delighted to discover that we had the whole place to
ourselves. On the walls were old hats, furs, and antique
jewelry. This was definitely a girlie-girl place, and we
couldn't wait to sip tea and talk to our hearts' content.
We laughed at the thought of our husbands sitting in this
place, but then we spotted an antique soldier's helmet. It
must be that some men dared to come in!

Before long, our charming waitress with a Southern drawl served a feast fit for a queen—homemade raspberry English scones, eggs, and fruit, with individual teapots and colorful cozies on an antique silver platter.

After breakfast, we took notice of the variety of hats on the walls. Before we knew it, we were out of our chairs, going from hat to hat to find the one that suited each of us best. Lisa chose a red velvet style, sleek to her head, with a veil that cloaked her gorgeous brown eyes. Chrissie popped on an Audrey Hepburn saucer-type white hat that looked adorable.

Suddenly, I realized we were without a camera. How could that be? The waitress sent me to a nearby shop to buy a disposable one, assuring me that we could capture the moments just fine. By the time I returned, Chrissie had wrapped a hot pink boa around her neck, and Lisa had donned an antique fur.

Snap! Snap! The waitress took shots of us in various poses. With each picture, our ever-increasing giggles bubbled to the surface. At one point, Chrissie, standing in front of the fireplace mantel that was laden with antique china teacups, flung her hot pink boa around her neck. Oops! It knocked over a precious teacup. The waitress captured the moment on

For the Record

The world's largest tea party, documented by the 2006 *Guinness Book of World Records,* was a simultaneous tea party in various locations throughout the United Kingdom.

A steaming cup of tea and tasty buns were enjoyed by 11,760 participants at the "Largest Tea and Buns" event organized by the Emergency Role of Sheltered Housing organization in the U.K.

camera, with Chrissie's mouth and eyes wide open.

When we returned to our condo, the guys teased us by saying that we were too old to play dress-up. The three of us looked at each other and smiled. We knew in our hearts what had happened during those hours. It was a girl thing, and we connected on a level that we hadn't for years. Months later, I still can't look at those tea-party photos without laughing out loud.

Sherrie Eldridge

Steeped in Cherished Memories

We meet to create memories
and part to cherish them.

Indian Proverb

N ot long ago, I went to visit my elderly Aunt Mary who lives in a nursing home. Alzheimer's disease had taken its toll. As I sat beside her, my aunt stared vacantly into space, her once vibrant features frozen into an unhappy frown. She hardly glanced at the bouquet of daisies I had brought, and when I tried to take her hand, she pulled away from me in fright. I felt a terrible sense of loss, remembering how close we had been and the confidences we had shared through the years, usually over a cup of tea in her cozy kitchen.

As a very young girl, I loved to visit Aunt Mary. Childless herself, she had time and energy to lavish on a favorite niece. My favorite spot was a chair at her kitchen table where she always served me tea, sometimes accompanied by her Irish soda bread, thick with plump raisins and sprinkled with caraway seeds. She made an elegant ceremony out of our teas, covering the table with her snowy Irish linen tablecloth and putting out her finest china cups. As we drank our tea, she listened intently to my stories about school and my worries about friendship. No one else in my young life took me as seriously. Sometimes she would tell me tales of her childhood on a farm in Ireland, her fears on her journey to America over a storm-tossed ocean, her struggles as a young immigrant girl seeking work in a big city.

Aunt Mary taught me many things—how to take up a hem, how to write a thank-you note, and, most important of all, how to make a proper pot of tea. First, she told me, you put on the kettle, and just before the water comes to a boil, you fill the teapot halfway with hot water to warm it. When the kettle boils, you keep it simmering while you throw out the water in the teapot, and then put in a level spoonful of tea leaves—one for each person and one for the pot. After you add the boiling water, you let it steep for a few minutes. Then, before you serve it, you strain the leaves with care.

My aunt had a firm belief in the soothing powers of tea. Growing up, I had my share of adolescent misery. One snowy evening, I arrived at Aunt Mary's in tears over a broken romance. She helped me off with my coat, brushed the snow from my hair, and then said in a determined voice, "I'll put the kettle on."

I sat at her table in the kitchen and wiped my eyes. The sound of the kettle's singing whistle, the cheerful clatter of the dishes and silver as my aunt set the table, the sight of the white tablecloth with its embroidered green sham-rocks, all served to calm my shattered spirit. Soon, I was warming my cold hands around a steaming cup, strong and dark and fragrant.

"Drink your tea," my aunt admonished. I felt the blood returning to my face. The ritual soothed and reassured. Life goes on, it said. One day at a time.

As we sipped our tea, Aunt Mary spoke to me about her own heartbreak when her husband died. But she drew strength and solace from friends and family, just as I would, indeed as I was doing now, restored by my aunt's sympathetic attention. In those moments, my aunt taught me a vital lesson in the power of empathy—a lesson I remember to this day.

Then, as a special treat, Aunt Mary read me my fortune in the tea leaves.

"You'll be meeting someone new—a tall, handsome young man," she said, gazing into the bottom of my cup. Soon, we were giggling together.

"When?" I heard myself asking, the tears now dried on my face.

"Soon," she intoned, "very soon." I left her that day with a lighter heart and a head full of dreams.

I thought of that long-ago afternoon as I sat beside my aunt in the nursing home, wondering if I would ever connect with her again. I looked out the window. It was beginning to get dark. A long drive home awaited me. I would have to leave soon. Yet I was reluctant to go without even a sign of recognition from my aunt.

But then I remembered passing the kitchen on the way to Aunt Mary's room and seeing an ancient teapot on the stove. With the permission of the staff, I went into the kitchen and set about making afternoon tea. I found a tray and arranged it with the teapot, two cups and saucers, lemon, sugar, and cream. I placed all on a paper doily—not as elegant as Aunt Mary's tablecloth, but it would do. As a final touch, I added the daisies I had brought, putting them into a small vase.

"It's time for tea," I announced, as I carried the tray into my aunt's room. For the first time that day, there was a change in her facial expression. Her eyes widened with a look of pleased surprise. As I poured the tea and asked her old, familiar questions, "Lemon or cream? One sugar or two?" she suddenly reached for my hand and said, "Oh, my dear, how lovely."

It was as if the homely ritual with its associations of home and loved ones had awakened her dormant spirit. We might have been back together once again in her cozy kitchen. The bond between us could never be broken, I realized. We sat together then, sipping our tea, connected once more by the healing power of tea and sympathy.

Eileen Valinoti

🍵 older and wiser

Tea is the one beverage most commonly enjoyed by centenarians.

Researchers working in the United States have shown that green tea, with its high levels of antioxidants, can help reduce the risk of obesity, Alzheimer's disease, and many other disorders related to aging.

when Tinker Bell came to Tea

Whatever is lovely . . .
think about such things.

Philippians 4:8 NIV

I sat at the table, swinging my legs and watching dust motes dance in a bright shaft of afternoon sunlight. My baby sister, Bobbi, was down for her nap, and it was finally time for the promised tea party. I looked up as my mother came out of the kitchen carrying two steaming cups. "It's hot," she warned, setting mine in front of me. "Wait for the milk." She set her own cup right in the shaft of sunlight, then turned back to the kitchen.

I carefully blew on the weak brew that half-filled my cup. Since the birth of my sister, her nap was the only time I had my mother all to myself. Mom had always been great about turning off the vacuum to be the Wicked Witch to my Dorothy or setting aside her dusting cloth to take me outside to talk to the snapdragons in our garden, gently squeezing the blooms so that their mouths opened and closed. But since Bobbi's birth, there had been less time for make-believe.

Mom returned with a pink Melmac creamer full of milk, a matching sugar bowl, and a pink and white plate of the peanut-butter cookies I had helped her bake after Captain Kangaroo that morning. My job had been to dip a fork into flour and press it flat against the mounds of dough Mom dropped onto the cookie sheet. Bobbi had watched us from her highchair, too little to help.

Mom sat down across from me now and scooped two spoonfuls of sugar into my cup before filling it almost to the top with milk. She added only a few drops of Sweeta to hers. As we stirred our cups, Mom glanced at the ceiling. "Look at that!" she said. "Tinker Bell has come to visit."

I quickly put down my spoon and looked up. Sure enough, there was a bright spot of light dancing back and forth on our ceiling. I stared in awe. "Is it really Tinker Bell?"

Mom took a sip from her cup before setting it back on the table to reach for a cookie. Tinker Bell disappeared for a moment, then returned, more lively than ever. "It looks like her to me," Mom said.

"Hi, Tinker Bell! Do you want some tea?" When she did not come down for a sip, I bit into a cookie. What an exciting tea party! But then special things often happened on afternoons spent with my mother. I kept my eyes on the ceiling as much as possible until my cookie was gone and my cup was empty. Mom reached for her cup and swirled the dark liquid. "You'd better say good-bye to her," she advised. "She'll probably leave when our party is over."

I looked up at the bright fairy over our heads, not wanting the magic to end. "I want her to stay," I pleaded.

Mom continued to swirl the liquid in her cup as she, too, watched Tinker Bell dance. "She needs to get back to

Neverland to see Peter Pan. But I bet she'll be back again, honey," she soothed.

"Tomorrow?"

"Maybe not tomorrow." Mom glanced at the sunny window. "It's supposed to rain tomorrow. Fairies don't like rain."

"Okay." I was satisfied with that. My mother knew a lot about fairies and elves and giants and things. I looked toward the ceiling once more. "Good-bye, Tinker Bell," I told the light. "I hope you come to our tea party again." With one more series of darts back and forth, Tinker Bell disappeared. I lowered my eyes to watch my mother drain her teacup. "That was a fun tea party," I told her.

She grinned at me across the table. "Yes, it was."

My mother and I had lots more tea parties over the next year before I started school, and Tinker Bell was a guest at many of them. But Mom was right: she only seemed to show up on sunny afternoons. Many years later, Tink returned to join my little son and me at our tea parties, always on sunny days, of course. For everyone knows that while they adore tea parties, fairies don't come out when it rains.

Julia Miller

A Sweet (Tea) Story

All well-regulated families
set apart an hour every morning for
tea and bread and butter.

Joseph Addison

Sweet tea is to the Southern dinner table like Jimmy Carter is to peanuts. The two just go together. But on my Savannah, Georgia, dinner table, we always had unsweetened tea, probably because we used the instant kind. If you wanted sugar, you poured teaspoon after teaspoon into the murky, cold glass and stirred until it all dissolved. It was not sweet tea, not really. At least, not the kind you'd find in most Southern homes.

So I preferred my tea unsweetened. In fact, I never learned to like sweet tea. My husband-to-be, a young man from the small town of Sandersville, Georgia, thought I was crazy. What kind of true Southern gal drinks unsweetened tea? And instant tea, to boot. It's a wonder he stuck around long enough to marry me, but I suppose I had other charms.

His mother, however, didn't find me quite as charming. My mother-in-law was a cook-from-scratch kind of woman who started fixing the Saturday noon dinner at

7:30 in the morning. By the time I rolled out of bed, she'd have the green beans simmering in fatback and the beef roast in the oven. After I'd washed and dried my hair, it was 11:00 and time to set the table. By then, she'd have the rice and gravy ready, and the tea brewed and sweetened. The corn bread would go in, and every five minutes or so, till 12:00 on the dot, she'd jump up and run to the kitchen to check on something. Finally, she'd call, "Cathy, put the ice in the glasses and pour the tea," and we'd sit down to eat.

For nearly a year, I poured the sweet tea in my glass and politely sipped. My mother-in-law found it very amusing that anyone would drink instant tea. I was too embarrassed to admit that I drank it unsweetened. It was bad enough that I didn't know how to make real tea, or corn bread, or biscuits, or fry up a mess of chicken. I'm sure she thought her son would waste away, living with a cook like me. She tsk-tsked my lack of culinary experience, while I drank my share of unsweetened tea.

But I quickly learned how to brew tea. And wonder of wonders, my husband got used to unsweetened tea—so much so that he preferred it, too. It was just a matter of time before the tea became an issue when we visited Momma. Though, to my husband's credit, he tried to take the blame.

"Momma, I don't really like sweet tea anymore," said my husband one Saturday morning while his mother brewed the tea.

"What in the world? You've always liked sweet tea," said Momma.

"Well, now I don't. And besides, Cathy likes her tea unsweetened, too."

He probably shouldn't have added that last part because then I got "the look"—the look that said I'd corrupted her son in some unspeakable manner. This crazy, unsweetened tea business was clearly all my doing. Technically, I guess it was. I looked all over that kitchen, trying to appear innocent. But I sure didn't look at my mother-in-law.

So, that very day, my husband's mother set two pitchers on the table. The large pitcher held sweet tea. A small pitcher, which held maybe two glasses of tea, was unsweetened. By the end of dinner, the small pitcher was empty. The large pitcher sat on the table, nearly untouched. But it was a start.

Eventually, my mother-in-law shared her cooking expertise with me. I learned how to make caramel icing with toasted pecans, though not as well as she did. I even learned how to make skillet corn bread that browned on the edges and was perfect for sopping up all those delicious vegetables.

Then one day, right about noon, my mother-in-law called, "Cathy, put the ice in the glasses and pour the tea." To the counter I went for the small pitcher. But there was only one pitcher on the counter: the large pitcher, filled to the brim with unsweetened tea. I didn't know that a pitcher could talk, but that day, I'm sure I heard that unsweetened tea say loud and clear, "Welcome home, Cathy."

Cathy C. Hall

America's Contribution

The only commercial tea plantation in North America is the Charleston Tea Plantation, which produces American Classic brand tea.

R. C. Bigelow, Inc., the Connecticut tea company, purchased the South Carolina plantation at auction in 2003. The property is located about twenty miles west of Charleston on rural Wadmalaw Island.

Tea at the Charleston plantation is harvested from late April through October. The public is welcome, and free tours allow visitors to walk through the plant, see the equipment, and learn how tea is made from crop to cup.

Tea for Three

Tea is a cup of life.

Author Unknown

"I'm going to invite another woman to your baby shower," my friend Candace told me. "You don't have anything in common with her, but she lives just down the block and is pregnant, too."

"Fine," I said, curious about this woman I would have nothing in common with except pregnancy. That seemed like enough. Everyone else in the neighborhood was working, and the days were lonely.

Jenny came to the shower. She was about six months behind me in her pregnancy and also lonely at home all day. After the shower, we agreed to meet for tea. For as long as I can remember, a cup of tea has been my comforter, picker-upper, and calmer-downer. Whatever the problem, a cup of tea will take the edge off and allow me to go on.

My tea dates with Jenny became almost daily rituals as we got to know each other and found out how much we did have in common. We each had two older children—a boy and a girl—besides the ones we were expecting. She was a graduate of the college I was attending part-time, and we were both English majors. That meant books were a favorite topic of conversation and sharing.

For many years, Jenny remained my tea-drinking buddy. As our friendship continued to blossom, we developed many more similar interests—all shared over a cup of tea. The tea we sipped during our pregnancies with my daughter, Cathy, and her son, Corey, led to cups of tea shared as we sat in the shade of the elm tree in my back-yard while the kids played in the sandbox and wading pool. We enjoyed a cup under her weeping willow as they climbed into its branches. In the winter, cups of tea warmed us as we watched the kids sledding down our steep driveway. The two seemed to have as much in com-mon as we did. They shared the middle name Dale, enjoyed each other's birthday parties, completed art proj-ects together, and helped each other with homework as Jenny and I drank tea and shared our lives.

When Cathy and Corey were ten, Jenny announced her husband's job was taking their family to another state. With heavy hearts, we packed their belongings into our pickup and helped them move.

Later, we shared a last cup of tea in their new home, and I drove back to mine wondering when, where, or how I would ever find another tea buddy. Everyone else I knew was working full-time and didn't have the time for or interest in tea.

Jenny and I kept in touch with letters—real letters on stationery, not e-mails or text messages. We would sit down with a cup of tea to write the letter and then later make a cup of tea to drink as we read the letter we got back. It wasn't as good as meeting in person, but it kept us connected through good times and bad—our daughters' weddings, my breast cancer, her husband's illness, Corey's near death from a home-invasion shooting that left him paralyzed, and my Cathy's diagnosis of multiple sclerosis. I was grateful for the support I received from her, but I still longed for another woman on the other side of the teapot.

Jenny had found a friend in her new community who shared tea with her. I was happy for her, but a little jealous. Then I moved to a new community, too. I met many nice people, but they all drank coffee, and no one seemed to have the time or inclination to sit down and sip a leisurely cup of tea. One day after church, as everyone was sharing in coffee hour, I noticed a woman wiping off a dusty kettle, filling it with water, and setting it on the stove. I walked up to her.

"I just felt like a cup of tea today," she said. "Sometimes it hits the spot better than coffee."

"I know," I said. "May I join you?"

Thus began my second satisfying tea relationship. Martha had so much in common with Jenny, and therefore with me, that I couldn't believe it. It wasn't only tea we shared. We all three loved to shop at thrift stores, and reuse and recycle whatever we could. We were gardeners. We all had children we had stayed home to raise. We now had adult married children. We loved books and reading.

Martha and I never ran out of things to discuss over the teapot. I felt at home at her dining-room table as the steam from the tea mingled with our conversations. My tea-life would have been perfect if only Jenny and Martha could meet. But Jenny was still in Arizona, and we were still in Colorado.

Then Jenny came for a visit. She agreed to come with me to church and the potluck afterward. Finally, Jenny and Martha met, and the tea-threesome was complete. I couldn't imagine anything more fun than sharing tea with the two of them and watching them learn to appreciate each other as I appreciate each of them. Tea for two is fine, but tea for three is wonderful.

Jean Campion

How to Brew a Great Cup of Tea

● The best way to brew black or oolong tea is to use fresh, cold water that has just started to boil. Green tea should be brewed with water that has not yet come to a full boil (or water that has boiled, and then been set aside and cooled for a few minutes). Reheated water gives tea a flat taste, so always use fresh water. Don't let the water boil more than a few seconds. If you boil it too long, it loses its oxygen and makes the tea taste bitter.

● Use one teaspoonful of loose tea or one tea bag per cup. If you like your tea weaker or stronger, adjust that ratio. Pour the "just-boiling" water over the tea.

● Brew the tea 3–5 minutes. Don't judge the strength of tea by its color. It takes 3–5 minutes for the tea leaves to unfold and release their flavor.

● Sugar, honey, or sweetener bring out the flavor of flavored teas. The English use milk in their tea. Some people enjoy cream or half-and-half. In Malaysia and other Asian countries, sweetened condensed milk is used liberally in tea for a rich dessert-like beverage. Heavy cream can mask the flavor of the tea.

● To make a whole pot of tea for guests, fill a decorative teapot with hot tap water to warm it while your water is coming to a boil on the stove. Then pour the hot water out of the pot and replace it with the just-boiling water. Add loose tea to the pot, one teaspoon per cup, and let it float around the pot for 3–5 minutes. Then pour the tea through a strainer right into the cups of your guests. Decorative tea strainers can sit right on top of a cup. If the tea is kept in the water too long, it will become bitter, so if you plan to make a large pot to last during a tea party, use tea bags so they can be removed easily after brewing.

compassion and a cannoli

My dear, if you could
give me a cup of tea to clear
my muddle of a head, I should better
understand your affairs.

Charles Dickens

I grew up in a house where coffee was the strength of rocket fuel, and everyone drank it black. The only experiences I'd had with tea were the rare requests on holidays from one elderly aunt.

In college, I worked as a waitress in a small café on MacDougal Street in Greenwich Village. Inside the café I felt as if I'd left Manhattan. There were Renaissance-style paintings on the walls, chairs with iron backs with curlicue designs, big black and white floor tiles, and a ceiling made of stamped tin with a diamond pattern.

My boss, Pepe, wore a white apron tied around his waist, and his round belly rolled over the top. He wore black Keds and jeans. His T-shirts were red, green, or white—the colors of the Italian flag. He taught me how to put the cream in the cannolis by holding my hand in the same way my father had when he'd guided me through cutting a steak.

On my first day, Pepe directed me to the tea boxes. They took up two shelves behind the espresso machine. They were a parade of rainbow colors—Darjeeling, English Breakfast, Earl Grey, Jasmine, Peach, Vanilla Almond, Hazelnut, and Green—and an array of decaf choices, many with the same names, plus Peppermint and Chamomile.

I asked Pepe, "Why so many teas? Does anybody actually order tea?"

He laughed and said, "You must be Italian. Italians drink espresso, but everybody else . . ." Pepe shrugged and rolled his eyes.

We had a regular customer in the café, a man in his early fifties. His thick glasses had heavy dark frames that were too big for his face. They magnified his hazel eyes. He always wore a khaki trench coat and smelled musty, as if he lived in an attic. He always chose the table in the corner by the window. He'd take off his trench coat, fold it neatly, and place it over the chair across from him. I think he thought of that trench coat as the friend he was dining with. If his table was already taken, he'd break out in a sweat, and his magnified eyes would dart around the room. Usually, he'd wait for his table, except on rare occasions when I told him that folks had just sat down and it would be a long wait.

I'd bring him the tall, glossy menu, and he'd study it intently with his wacky glasses. I'd look over at him now and then. Finally, he'd close the menu, push it in front of him, and stare at his napkin. He'd move the salt and pepper shakers into position like defensive pawns in a chess game. He always ordered the same thing—an Earl Grey tea and a cannoli. I'd ask him if he wanted milk or lemon with the tea. He always paused as if carefully considering these options and then he'd reply politely, "No, thank you."

When I put down the tea and pastry, his posture changed. He'd sit up a little straighter, hold his head a little higher. He'd pick up the teacup, put it right under his nose, and inhale deeply. His face lost its tension. He'd pull the tea bag out of the cup and place it in his spoon. He'd wrap the white string around and lift the spoon three times, forcing a few drops of tea into the cup. He'd set down the spoon with the tea bag on his napkin. He'd curl his hands around the warm cup. He'd then switch over to the cannoli. He was the only customer who used a knife and fork. Everybody else just picked up a cannoli like a hot dog.

I secretly named him Norman, after Norman Bates in the movie, *Psycho*. It was not because he frightened me, or seemed capable of killing a woman in a shower, but because he seemed like a man who'd always lived with his mother and rarely ventured out into the world.

One day, I decided to surprise Norman. I was tired of our silly ritual of me bringing the menu as if Norman had to think about what he was going to order. I wanted him to know that I knew him so well that I could bring him exactly what he wanted without him uttering a word, like in movies when the main character calls out to the waitress, "I'll have the usual." I wanted him to feel special.

As Norman folded his trench coat and placed it in its

spot over the chair across from him, I was already at the counter.

"Pepe, gimme an Earl Grey and a cannoli."

Pepe, knowing full well that our Norman always took his tea plain, winked at me and said, "Lemon or milk?" I giggled and picked up my order. I bounced over with my twenty-one-year-old spring in my step and proudly placed the tea and pastry in front of Norman with a big, proud smile. Norman broke out in a horrible sweat, far worse than the sweating when his corner seat was occupied. Poor Norman's hands started to shake. He began to rock back and forth in the seat and mutter words too quiet for me to make out. He looked up at me the way a child would if I told him I'd given away the family dog.

"I'm so sorry," I said, "I thought it would make you happy if I surprised you."

Norman replied in a whisper, "No, no, no. Please don't do that."

I nodded my head and silently gave Norman my solemn vow that I would never, ever do that again. Norman pushed the salt and pepper shakers into position. The following day when Norman arrived, I pretended not to see him. I wanted to give him privacy and time to meticulously fold his trench coat, lovingly drape it over the chair, sit down in the wooden chair by the window, and get his bearings. When he looked comfortable, I walked over to Norman with a menu and said, "Good morning," trying to sound nonchalant.

Norman took the menu and began to study it through his big, thick glasses. I trotted off to answer the calls of my other customers. After I made my rounds, I returned to Norman in his neat and tidy corner with the folded menu and the salt and pepper chess pieces poised in position.

"What can I get you today?" I asked.

"Earl Grey tea and a cannoli," Norman said without looking up.

"Would you like lemon or milk with that?"

"No, thank you," he said.

I smiled, took the menu, and walked over to the counter, relieved that Norman was happy again and that he had at least one friend in the world—his waitress.

Dorri Olds

The Soothing Elements of Tea

The tea party is a spa
for the soul. You leave your cares
and work behind. Busy people forget
their business. Your stress melts away,
your senses awaken.

Alexandra Stoddard

"You're Invited to a Tea to Celebrate Janet's Birthday"
read the invitation that my mom had artistically
prepared for my tenth birthday celebration.

Bursting with excitement, I raced down the narrow dirt
streets of my hometown of La Paz, Bolivia, to deliver them
to each of my neighborhood friends. The common tradition of enjoying an afternoon cup of tea became special
when it included a birthday celebration.

As in most Latin American countries, drinking tea
begins at the dawn of life. My grandmother prepared
anise tea and poured it into a baby bottle to ease nagging
colic in little family members. She grew a myriad of
plants, whose leaves she used to prepare tea. According
to her, each leaf or herb held special properties to cure
any ailment imaginable. Perhaps it was the love she
exuded when she handed us the aromatic blend that

eased the afflictions we experienced.

As part of her daily routine, wearing her apron over her black wool skirt, Grandmother stood in the doorway looking outside as her echoing voice called us in for mid-afternoon tea. Missing this important treat would leave us famished until dinner, which wasn't served until 8:30 in the evening.

Engraved in my heart are memories of so many afternoon teas. I can still smell the warm golden bread at the center of the table. Beside it sat a plate of white homemade cheese and a glass bowl of Grandmother's orange marmalade. And while we sipped our tea, the conversations with her added a special delight for me.

During the school year, once the dismissal bell rang, I dashed out and headed to the corner bus stop. I would wiggle my way through the crowded old bus and sit clutching my book bag, gazing out the window at the activity on the streets. Vendors in their colorful garb sat behind their stands, calling out their wares to the crowds who jammed the sidewalks. Then I would elbow my way out of the bus and hop off with anticipation thumping in my heart. My gaze would travel past the green lawn to the tall building, the only university in La Paz, where Mom worked in the basement cataloging books. I darted as quickly as my young legs would take me through the large entrance, pushed the glass door that opened into the library, and headed down the stairs to the basement. As I slipped between tall bookshelves, the smell of buttery pastries wafted straight to my growling stomach. Swinging the door open, and with a huge grin, my gaze swept through the familiar scenery—my mom and her colleagues' chatter blending with the pleasant aroma of coffee, tea, and cream. After breaking loose from Mom's tight hug, I glanced at the mound of flaky pastries on the table along the wall.

But, as afternoon tea breaks offered moments of relaxation for all, Bolivia's unstable government and stagnant economy offered scarce opportunities for my brother and me.

Two years later in 1964, while seated in our tiny, dark kitchen, it was time for our daily tea time again. With Mom stirring sugar in her cup, I watched as she gazed toward my grandmother and announced her decision to move to America. Grandma set her cup on the saucer with a loud clank, and tears flowed down her wrinkled cheeks. My grandfather, who had lost his lucidness along with most of his teeth, sat in silence, and with shaky hands, dunked his crusty bread into his tea.

After we began our life in America, whether by design or coincidence, I found special moments over cups of tea. When I lost my sight to an incurable retinal disease, my mom and I would sit sipping tea in the cozy kitchen of her condo. She reassured me that I wasn't alone in my darkness. The aroma of the citrus blend still lingers, as do her words echoing in my heart: God would provide, and she would be my eyes.

God did provide. At times, while the family slept, I sat in silence with a cup of herbal tea, pondering just how much he had granted me. His provision included Mom's perennial assistance, and a renewed attitude, confidence, and determination on my part. With the aid of a computer program that reads the screen, I'm able to string together words of inspiration for those who might need a little light in the midst of dark moments.

As herbal tea comes in a variety of flavors, different types of events also came into my life. When my heart was sliced with pain after losing my nineteen-year-old son, in the midst of cold anguish, I remember moments of warm comfort. My mom handed me a cup of chamomile tea with honey. "Here, sweetheart," she said. "It's okay to cry. God knows your pain, and he will heal your heart."

Now, as I take the last sip of my Lady Grey tea, I set the cup on the corner of my desk, and the eyes of my heart review the scenery of my life. Fueled by gratitude, my fingers begin to dance on the keyboard, relating the blend of emotions that swirl in my heart like tea leaves in the cup.

Janet Perez Eckles

American Ingenuity

It's been said that the Boston Tea Party was responsible for the development of herbal teas in the United States.

Because England was imposing such high taxes on imported tea, the American farmers concocted their own blends of local herbs, flowers, fruits, and spices, combining leaves, roots, bark, seeds or flowers of other plants (not the tea plant). Herbal teas are still made this way today, all over the world.

Unfortunately, although an enjoyable and soothing drink, herbal teas have not been proven (yet!) to impart the medicinal benefits linked to traditional black, oolong, green, and white teas.

My First Tea

I am in no way interested in immortality,
but only in the taste of tea.

Lu T'ung

I remember my first tea. It took place in my back-yard. On a bright spring day with flowers bloom-ing and the birds singing a lively tune, I commandeered a wooden crate for a makeshift table, turn-ing it upside-down. Throwing a small red-and-white-checked piece of cloth over the top, I began smoothing it with my hands, making sure it hung just right on all sides. I was excited. My first tea was about to begin.

In the center of the table, I placed a small vase spilling over with wildflowers picked from my backyard. The flow-ers, the colors of spring, were sweet smelling and reminded me of perfume my mama sometimes wore. They were per-fect for my first tea. Sitting beside the table, inside a minia-ture brown wicker trunk, a fine china tea set was nestled snug in silk-covered straw. Picking up a cup, I tipped it toward the light. I could see the tiny imprinted words "bone china" through the milky-white bottom of the teacup. "It's a sure sign of fine china," Mama said. "When you have a tea, only your best china should be used."

One by one, I lifted the delicate pieces painted with red roses, green leaves, and vines, and placed each piece carefully and just so on the checkered cloth. The creamer with milk, the bowl full of sugar cubes, a small chocolate cake, and the teapot filled with warm Earl Grey finished the setting. Now everything was ready.

Soon, my guests began to arrive and sat upon the ground around the table with the checkered cloth. Veronica was first and sat primly to my left. Looking particularly fetching in a pink satin dress with ecru lace, she sported a jaunty matching bonnet on top of her tight strawberry curls. I arranged the skirt of her dress around her to keep it from being soiled. Kay arrived next, and she was lovely, wearing a white bonnet over her sandy brown hair. A baby-blue-and-white-striped pinafore with embroidered pink flowers covered the powder-blue organza dress she wore, bringing out the deep crystal-blue of her eyes. Suzy, last to arrive, sat across from me, hatless but striking with her long, golden ringlets hanging to her waist. The thick white satin jacket with gold trim and loops of gold braids hanging from her left shoulder looked especially nice with the white pleated skirt she had chosen to wear.

I had slipped on a spring dress with a soft wispy skirt, borrowed from my mama. After using a bobby pin to pull my wavy blonde hair away from my face, I put a pink pill-box hat with thin netting, hanging at the edge of my eyes, on my head. I sat down, spreading the full skirt in a half-circle behind me. I hoped I looked as elegant as I felt. With everyone in place, my first tea began.

As hostess, I poured the golden brown liquid from the teapot into each dainty cup, adding just the right amount of sugar and cream. After placing tiny slices of chocolate cake on each plate, we began our tea. They all agreed it was delicious. It was nice to have time to relax and take pleasure in sipping a cup of tea and enjoying the lovely afternoon outdoors with friends. We laughed often, and the conversation became lively as we exchanged gossip and caught up on the general news of the week. However, the afternoon was fleeing fast, and all too soon, the cake was gone, the teapot was empty, and my first tea party was at an end. Before long, it was time to say our good-byes, but before they went inside, my guests and I agreed it was a delightful tea, and we would do it again soon.

Years have passed since I was seven and had my first tea with my dolls. Since that day, I've had many teas—some with my dolls, a few with my mama, many with friends. However, the one most vivid in my mind is that spring afternoon in my backyard celebrating my first tea.

Janice Olson

Grandmother's Tea

Tea is drunk to forget the din of the world.

T'ien Yiheng

A soothing scent of lavender candles lingered in the piano studio. Outside, snow danced in the cold, winter wind. Sipping my tea, I relaxed in my old wooden chair, focusing on Kate's long, slender fingers caressing the white keys of my black piano.

For some reason, she struggled. The emotion that usually flowed from her seemed absent. I wondered what could be bothering her. She'd been playing for eleven years. The last six had been here, so I knew her playing ability.

My fingertips automatically started to tap the waltzing rhythm on my armrest. As her song drew to a close, she inhaled a long breath, and played her final cadence while releasing her breath and tired hands.

"Kate, that was rhythmically beautiful. What do you think was missing?"

"Mrs. Monette, I just can't get into it today. Do you mind if I have a cup of your tea while we do our lesson? My throat is dry."

"Sure. Why don't you try the new Mozart piece while I get it for you?" We often shared a cup of tea during her lessons, so it wasn't an unusual request. Regardless, I couldn't help thinking something was wrong.

The sound of Mozart trying to escape from my piano interrupted my thoughts. Releasing a sigh under my breath, I muttered, "Poor girl."

Upon returning to the studio, the music subsided. "Here you go. Have a drink, then we will continue."

"Thank you, Mrs. Monette. I really enjoy tea." She took a drink and paused to contemplate saying more, but nothing verbalized.

"Is everything all right, Kate?" Worry and sadness settled deep into her eyes. Nothing but silence filled the room as she took another drink of tea. Rising from my chair to grab the brown technique book, I gently rubbed her arm.

"Remember, Kate, I am always here for you." We managed to finish all of the scales and pieces that needed working on. At the end of the lesson, she deposited her books into her music bag and placed it on the bench.

I felt relieved as Kate seemed more at ease. She then did something a little unusual: she embraced me as you would a best friend you haven't seen in years. As I hugged her in return, she whispered, "Thank you, Mrs. Monette, thank you." I became speechless as she grabbed her bag and waved good-bye.

During my next three lessons, I couldn't stop wondering about Kate. My mind struggled with many different scenarios. What was bothering her? When my lessons were over, I snuffed out the candles and closed the studio door. With my teacup, now cold, I curled up in my over-sized sofa chair to enjoy the living room's silence. Circling the teacup's rim with my finger, I thought about Kate.

The rest of the week continued as usual until Saturday. Kate's father called. She would not be attending Monday's lesson. After the extensive call, I understood what had been bothering Kate. Her grandmother had fallen deathly ill the weekend prior to her previous lesson, and unfortunately, she had just passed away Friday, the day before Kate's father's call.

Poor thing. *If I'd only known,* I thought. During my first lesson the following Thursday, the telephone rang.

"Hello, Mrs. Monette?"

"Hello. Kate, is that you?"

"Yes, I'm wondering . . . when are you done teaching today?"

"Well, at five-thirty. Why?" I only heard silence from Kate's end.

Why would she hang up? I questioned under my breath.

After I escorted my last student of the day out of the house, I shut the door and turned the lock. Stopping to pick up some books from the floor, I heard a shuffling on the front step.

As I turned on the outside light, a faint little knock sounded on the wooden door. I opened the door, and there stood Kate. She had tears frozen to her rosy cheeks and a brown paper bag in her left arm.

"Come in, girl! How long have you been out there?"

She handed me the bag. "Can we have a cup of tea?"

Looking in the bag, I saw a box of peppermint tea. My gaze met hers, and she began to weep. "Every day after supper, I would have peppermint tea with my grand-mother . . ." She struggled with her words between sobs. Embracing her, I calmly whispered, "Come, let's get some water on."

That evening, over peppermint tea, Kate shared stories about her grandmother. I felt grateful knowing our tea together began to comfort her sudden loss.

Amanda Monette

Tea Varieties to Enjoy

Formosa Oolong—grown on small family farms in Taiwan. It often has a slightly peachy flavor.

Earl Grey—a blend of black teas best known for its distinctive flavor because of the oil of bergamot, an Italian citrus fruit, added during processing.

Darjeeling—the champagne of teas. The flavor has been described as that of black currants or muscat grapes. Grown in Darjeeling, India, high in the Himalayan mountains near Nepal, it is considered a lighter afternoon tea, but it depends on the time of year the leaves are harvested.

Ceylon—any tea grown in Sri Lanka. Sir Thomas Lipton built his tea plantations and his fortune in Sri Lanka. The quality varies, but the best are full of fragrance and flavor because they are grown at high elevations.

English Breakfast—a blend of strong black teas from India and Sri Lanka (Ceylon). It makes a great wake-me-up tea full of interesting flavors.

Assam—discovered in the northeastern Indian province of Assam by a Scotsman in the 1830s. Until then, all tea came to the West from China. Assam tea is pungent, hearty, and dark in color.

Gunpowder—has a delicate and subtle flavor and fragrance, in spite of its name. It is a Chinese green tea in which each leaf from the tea plant has been rolled tightly right after being picked. The tighter the roll, the more expensive the tea.

Jasmine—a blend of black and green tea, or sometimes just green tea, with jasmine flowers added.

A Teahouse Drenched in Sunlight

An old man drinks tea
and reads the newspaper—
forgetting age for a moment.

Mason Cooley

T he entire teahouse was drenched in warm sunlight. Early morning shadows were cast about the room, falling off tables and climbing walls, making intricate patterns over people's faces. The room was full of Kurdish men who could not help but exude manliness. They read newspapers, fingered their mustaches, and took long draws on their cigarettes. They also devoted some time to staring at me, a solitary Westerner writing his notes.

Between sips of tea, I stared back, my eyes squinting in the bright light and not at all inclined to blink. Perhaps I stared because, with a scraggly two-month-old beard sprouting from my face, I, too, was feeling manly. Or maybe I stared because here in southeastern Turkey, staring just seemed to be the thing to do. Whatever the reason, the room was thick with sunlight and stares.

After some minutes, I offered a slight nod. And in slow-motion unison, they nodded in return, not once breaking their piercing gazes. The teahouse in which I sat was in Diyarbakir, a city situated on the banks of the Tigris River and home to hundreds of thousands of Kurds. But in three weeks I would leave all this behind and return to the United States, finally completing what had so far been a thirteen-month journey across Asia.

Along the way, I had grown accustomed to different foods and languages. I had grown accustomed to stares, to uncomfortable beds, and to the unknown. I had grown accustomed to feeling rugged. But I had grown accustomed to something else as well—something much more valuable than ruggedness, something that often left me humbled. You could call it the hospitality of locals toward a stranger.

The hospitality had come in a thousand ways. It had come, for example, in the form of a Chinese man offering me a cup of green tea as our train sped through the countryside at dawn. It had come in the form of a Malay university professor pouring me a cup of Cameron Highlands tea in his apartment in Kuala Lumpur. It had come in the form of a fellow passenger in Pakistan, handing me a cup of milk tea at a bus stop before even telling me his name. And now that I was in southeastern Turkey, exchanging a strong and silent gaze with Kurdish patrons of a teahouse, it was about to come to me again.

With my cup finished and my schedule demanding that I begin to leave the cozy confines of the teahouse, I drifted through the haze of a dozen men's cigarette smoke and stepped up to the counter to pay my tab. But the man behind the counter smiled and shook his head, refusing to take my money. Someone else—one of the men with whom I had exchanged stares, someone whom I would never know because he had already left—had paid the bill.

Joel A. Carillet

Tea'd Off

Tea with us became more than
an idealization of the form of drinking;
it is a religion of the art of life.

Okakura Kakuzo

I like tea as much as the next guy—unless the next guy is my husband. I believe green tea will decrease my chances of getting cancer, black will give a kick-start to my day, peppermint will settle my stomach, and chamomile will help me relax. So I make sure I prepare myself a cup of some kind at least twice a week. My husband, on the other hand, invariably chooses two bags, one green and one black, for every cup, and makes sure he has this brew many times each day. It may sound judgmental, but I have to say that my husband is a full-on tea addict.

One might say that tea is a good addiction, as addictions go. It is, after all, the drink of royalty according to the Internet. Discovered by a Chinese emperor 5,000 years ago, tea was given imperial sponsorship almost instantly upon its introduction to Japan in the sixteenth century. It became the rage among the European aristocracy about the same time it hit Japan, and filtered down through the classes to become a common household word and desire.

However, rage across Europe is not to be confused with the rage that flares in me when I find a cup or mug of tea creating yet another white circle on a favorite piece of furniture. Or when we are already late to meet friends and Ray must make a cup of tea before we leave.

I know that tea has been elevated to an art form in the gracious, exacting Japanese Tea Ceremony and in the special form of architecture developed for the building of teahouses here and abroad. But a tall, insulated brown cup from Starbucks does not look good on top of our piano alongside the glass box that holds an antique Japanese doll or the arrangement of several deep blue, delicately painted vases from China.

Although tea once filled the cargo holds of clippers, and then steamships plying between Holland or Britain and China, I personally don't believe a sloshing cup of the stuff needs to accompany Ray and me on every road trip. Ray believes that any outing, whether a five-minute drive to the market or a two-hour drive to favorite hiking trails, requires fortification with a cup of tea. One could argue that tea in the car is no problem because so many cups are now available with dependable lids. However, Ray is addicted to the beverage, not the act of finding and fastening down lids. While covers on cups are a fairly rare phenomenon around here, stains on floor mats and upholstered seat covers are not.

Ah, yes. Just as tea is the national drink in Russia along with vodka, it is the national drink in our house along with a good merlot.

So, how do I deal with all this? For quite a while, I didn't. Then, several days ago, when I heard the teakettle whistle, a bolt of anger shot through me. Its strength caught my attention. Did disruptions to my life caused by Ray's love of tea justify such a response?

I thought hard about it. Ray could be drinking straight scotch. He could be gambling away the mortgage on our house. He could be having an affair with a woman, not a cup of tea. I could quite possibly be overreacting.

In case you live with a tea addict, here's what I've decided. It would be extreme to instigate a Boston Tea Party here and dump out Ray's boxes and boxes of tea. Considering the fact that he cooks dinner more often than I do, and cleans up afterward, I could make a run through the house twice a day picking up teacups from the garage, bathroom counter, living-room windowsill, laundry-room dryer, and bedroom dresser, and still be spending less time helping out than he does. To prevent marks on the furniture, I could leave out a lot more coasters. In fact, perhaps his ubiquitous cups of tea are just what I need to justify a shopping spree—a little burnished wood here, a little sterling silver there. I might buy a nice canister for tea bags to set on the counter while I'm at it and free up

Best-Kept Secrets

Teas, like fine wines, possess qualities that reflect where they are grown. Many factors affect the quality and taste of the tea leaves, including altitude, climate, soil, and rainfall.

Twenty-five or thirty different tea blends may go into a specific brand of tea. The combinations are a closely guarded secret at most tea companies.

some storage space in the cupboard. As to the spills in the car, Ray grabs the first cup he finds on the shelf, so I could take five minutes to put the ones with screw-on lids well in front of the others.

Yes, tea is a good addiction as addictions go. It's also very pleasant to share. So rather than looking askance at Ray's next cup of tea, maybe I should pour myself a cup, too.

Samantha Ducloux Waltz

Tea for the Soul

We can survive functional
illiteracy or shattered windows of
vulnerability, but not the demise
of The Decent Cup of Tea.

Malachi McCormick

T hick snow lay on the ground when I came home
from the hospital. The city was almost crippled by
the unexpected blizzard. Winter had also engulfed
my soul—harsh and paralyzing. I had fractured my right
hip due to a tumor and had to have a hip replacement.

"You'll have radiation, a round of chemotherapy, and
two periods of stem-cell transplants. We'll harvest the
stem cells from you," my physician advised ominously.

My world had spun around, leaving me angry and
extremely frightened. Once a busy, practicing physician
who loved to travel, I had become, in an instant, an individual who felt helpless, unable to drive and earn a living.

My future looked bleak and uncertain.

The health agency sent me a caregiver to help me out
temporarily. She was a young nursing student who had to
leave school for financial reasons. I barely acknowledged
her presence. I was too immersed in self-pity and fear.

I went through my daily routine—meals and showers, interspersed with naptime and exercise—without any enthusiasm. I was moving around in a haze. Friends tried to cheer me up. My children devised ways to buoy up my spirits without success. I had retreated from the world.

One cold morning, my caregiver said, "My grandmother believed in the healing power of tea. She made lots of it at home." She offered me a cup and said, "Do you want to try it?"

I took two sips and handed the cup back to her. "I think I'll just take a nap."

As the days went by, my caregiver managed to include tea time in my daily routine. She'd prepare a cup for me each morning at 9:00 along with some crackers or cookies. She began to tell me stories about her family, of her dreams, of her frustrations, and of her strong belief in a Higher Power. I began to tell her something of myself, too, voicing out the pain in my soul that had taken such a stronghold in me. Without knowing it, I was slowly reaching out again to another human being and shedding my self-imposed isolation.

I started to look forward to this tea time. It became my lifeline. I received comfort from that warm cup. As I slowly sipped my tea, the world stopped for a moment. It was my downtime, my break from the turbulence that had invaded my life.

Those two years were not easy. I went through a harrowing time with my cancer treatment. I can walk now without any aid and am able to drive again. I am enjoying my grandchildren and the company of my friends in a prayer group. Each day for me has become precious. Tea time has become part of it.

When the world becomes unsettling and negative thoughts tend to overwhelm me, I sit back, get my cup of tea, turn on some classical music, and wait for peace to engulf me once more.

Evelina M. Mabini

Thelma's Morning Tea

It's not the tea that makes
tea time special; it's the spirit
of the tea party.

Emilie Barnes, If Teacups Could Talk

helma Ritter was a stubborn old gal, probably the most stubborn customer who ever walked through my tea-room door. She sounded a bit feisty over the phone, but once we sat down to discuss her event, I was instantly charmed. She spoke quietly yet got straight to the point, and I quickly observed a certain wit and hint of mischievousness about her. Hovering somewhere around eighty years old, she explained a longstanding obligation to organize the annual Morning Tea for her women's Sunday school class, some thirty to forty members.

"We're looking for some place new this year," she told me. "And we can only afford to pay five dollars each. Something like fruit and muffins, hot tea, maybe some orange juice and some sort of hot dish . . . something really nice."

I paused to compose myself before expressing my apologies. Fully aware there were other restaurants where perhaps she could get a good hot breakfast for $3.99, I was hesitant to tell her we could not. Nor did I want to appear boastful by reminding her that she would be dining on fine bone china and sipping hot tea served from a silver teapot. Nor could I bring myself to mention the subject of gratuity as she gazed directly into my eyes. So I chose my words carefully and attempted to explain away the possibility of entertaining her entire class of lady friends.

But it didn't work. Refusing to take no for an answer, she suggested I think about it, saying she would call me later.

Now I was in a dilemma. I wanted to help her out (sweet dear that she was), but a quick calculation on paper put the whole affair beyond impossible. I just couldn't do it . . . not with the added expense of bringing in my staff three hours earlier than usual. Not to mention the starched linens and fresh flowers on every table, as was our tradition. Honestly, I wanted to . . . but I just couldn't do it.

Thelma got back to me, as promised, a few days later. I was awkward in trying to convince her that I could not do her party for five dollars each. She responded with silence so I rambled on, shooting her my rather expensive cost for the brunch, deliberately avoiding the discussion of tips or tax. After I had my say, she sweetly reminded me that all her friends were on a limited income and "to tell the truth, they just can't afford any more than five dollars." I could pretty much tell she had no earthly plans of going anywhere else (not this year) and not a hope in the world of paying more than her friends could afford.

As for me, I was caving. Truth be known, I had a gut feeling that she had already spent quite a bit of time in some prayer closet, praying up a storm that her annual Morning Tea would be a success. More seriously, I had a feeling that somebody up there might have just answered her prayer. Something told me this was not a good business deal, but my conscience whispered there was a higher principle at work. So, reluctantly I agreed to her request . . . at five dollars per person. I wanted to turn her down. Honestly, I wanted to . . . but I just couldn't do it.

Our staff was on alert for a full brunch and Morning Tea buffet, and the kitchen was hot and humid by 7:30 AM. Thelma and her friends arrived promptly at nine. First course was a fresh fruit cup, served at the table in stemmed crystal. Apricot scones and lavish bowls of whipped cream waited on a sideboard filled with assorted jams and honey alongside antique teacups. The buffet was extensive. Selections ranged from sweet-potato muffins to ham-and-cheese croissants. Also included were homemade crumpets with marmalade butter, crispy bacon, and a "to-die-for" hot egg dish with portabella mushrooms. Refills were nonstop from the multiple pots of freshly brewed tea. And, of course, there was orange juice, as requested.

The laughter and chatter died down just before eleven. One by one, they collected their pocketbooks and favors, heading for the door as full as could be. Thelma, ever the good hostess, hugged each class member as they said their good-byes. They, in turn, patted her on the back and gave her all the praise for yet another successful affair. And rightly so.

After the last guest had departed, Thelma sought me out. Sure that she was about to thank me and my staff for our hospitality, I was caught off guard when she smiled warmly and said, "Now, dear, you remember to hold a date for me next year!" She was a stubborn old gal. I had tried to turn her away. Honestly, I wanted to . . . but I just couldn't do it.

Charlotte A. Lanham

Hot-the-pot

Some tea drinkers prefer to use a decorative teapot and loose tea leaves dropped in for proper steeping. When poured into a teacup, the tea is strained to filter out the leaves. Many different kinds of strainers are available.

Before the *almost-boiling* water is poured into the decorative pot, a little hot water is added to warm it up. Hence the term "hot-the-pot."

A minute after the teapot is warmed, before the tea water and leaves are added, the hot-the-pot water is poured down the drain.

When making a single cup of tea, you can still hot-the-pot. Your tea will stay warmer longer. Simply fill your cup or mug with the hottest tap water you can get and let it sit there, warming your cup. When your tea water has almost boiled, pour your hot-the-pot water down the drain, add your tea bag and then the water from the kettle, and let it brew.

2

TICKLING THE TASTEBUDS

Tea Time in the Ozarks

The best quality tea must unfold like
a mist rising out of a ravine, gleam like a lake
touched by a zephyr, and be wet and soft
like a fine earth newly swept by rain.

Lu Yu

I t was a fine day for a drive in the Ozarks. Dagni and I had left Wichita fairly early, stopping both for breakfast and lunch. The flat-as-a-pancake terrain of Kansas had given way to Missouri's rolling foothills sometime around noon. Bounteous trees still clung onto their yellow, brown, and occasionally orange leaves.

Every fall, for I don't remember how long, Dagni and I trek to the hills—sometimes to a huge craft show in Arkansas, and sometimes, like this trip, to Branson to see the shows and theme park. It's usually the highlight of our year.

As we approached a don't-blink-now sort of town and the speed limit made whizzing by an impossibility, we noticed a sign beckoning us to pause at a quaint little restaurant/tea room on the left side of the road.

We stopped abruptly. Quaint was the catchword for

this trip. We should have toted a bumper sticker saying, "Caution: This Vehicle Brakes for Quaint."

A large gift shop overflowing with country curios and culinary specialties delighted our senses as we entered. The pungent aroma of cinnamon sticks and fresh ground coffee filled the room.

Shuffling over pine floors, we stopped every few steps to say things like, "Oh, look at this!" "How cute!" or "Read this!" But our appetites soon channeled us to the restaurant entrance where vintage tablecloths adorned odd-shaped tables, and shabby chic décor pampered our eyes like a visual spa.

The cashier waved her hand like a fan. "Sit wherever you like, ladies." She handed us menus as we passed by.

The room was empty, perhaps because it was late afternoon—too early for dinner and too late for lunch. I headed for a table next to the window. The floral tablecloth reminded me of one my grandmother used to own.

"Is this okay?" I asked Dagni.

"This is great," she answered, sitting in the chair across from me.

We simultaneously opened the delicate menus that were intertwined with mauve ribbon and lace.

"Everything looks delicious," I commented.

The waitress slowly approached our table. She was young, about eighteen, and dressed a bit sloppy, I thought, for a tea room.

"We'll both have tea," I said, smiling as I imagined the fine china, fancy teapot, and assortment of teas soon to be at our fingertips.

"Hot?" asked the waitress.

"Yes." *Of course,* I added in my thoughts.

"And how about we split the coconut pie?" Dagni gave me a questioning glance over the rim of her glasses.

"Sure," I answered. We always split the pie.

The waitress sauntered away, and Dagni and I chatted about Branson.

"Everyone says Shoji Tobuchi is great."

"Who?"

"The Japanese violinist."

The waitress leaned over my shoulder as she deposited two glasses of what looked like iced tea without the ice onto the wooden table.

"The pie will be right out," she called as she headed back toward the kitchen.

I stared at the glass in front of me for a few seconds. Then I looked up at Dagni, who also seemed captivated by the glass in front of her.

"What's this?"

"Umm, tea."

"Like, hot tea?"

She gave a little nervous laugh. "Yes, I'm pretty sure that's what it is."

I could feel my chest tightening and my lips clamp together like a primal reflex that I had no control over. I didn't know whether to laugh or throw a fit. Sure, this would be perfect material for Jay Leno's monologue—someday—but right now I really didn't feel like laughing.

Immediately, I began searching the room for the elusive waitress.

Dagni, always the kindhearted, nonconfrontational soul that she is, whispered, "No big deal. I'll drink it like this—it doesn't matter." She gave me a pleading look. "Don't say anything."

Despite Dagni's desire for peace, my anger and disappointment persisted.

"It does matter. This is a tea room, for crying out loud."

"Shhhh! Don't let her hear you. She's probably new and doesn't know any better."

Dagni took a sip of the tea that she later admitted was barely lukewarm. But all she said then was, "It's fine."

I think some people come into our lives for a reason. They balance us out. They temper us. They teach us how to be better people. In this case, my friend, Dagni, taught me a lesson on how to treat others—with mercy and patience and dignity.

Suddenly, it was as if my life were flashing before my very eyes. I was nineteen years old and working as a waitress at a very exclusive country club in New York. The manager needed me to run an errand, and I missed out on the preview of the night's menu specials. One of the specials was an expensive cut of steak. I waited on a table where a very influential man and his wife were entertaining a group of friends, perhaps clients. He ordered the special steak for all of them.

When I put in the order, I failed to specify which ones, and out came the steaks—that is, chopped steaks. What did I know? I was only nineteen. Without realizing my mistake, I delivered them to the table. The man was furious. I was mortified. I will never forget the way he belittled and humiliated me in front of all those people. I felt like such a fool.

I looked up at Dagni and shook my head. "I know it's a mistake, but someone has to tell her about it."

I could see Dagni cringing as I waved the girl over to our table. She knew how bold and straightforward I could be.

"You know," I began in a very sweet voice, "instead of these glasses, I think maybe there might be some teacups and a teapot somewhere. And probably an assortment of tea bags. I bet nobody told you where they are."

"Oh, I'm so sorry. This is my first day on the job, and I couldn't find any in the kitchen, and nobody is around . . . but just a minute."

She scooped up both glasses and was gone in a flash.

"See, I wasn't nasty, not even sarcastic."

Dagni nodded in agreement. "No, you were very nice about it."

In a few minutes, our waitress returned to the table with a tray on which sat two Victorian teacups, a paisley teapot, and a variety of gourmet tea bags.

"Oh, how nice. Now isn't that pretty," chimed Dagni.

The waitress sighed. "I had no idea. Janet from the gift shop showed me where the teapots and cups are. I'm really sorry. I used the hot tea from the iced-tea machine. That was really dumb of me."

"No, no. It was just a mistake." I smiled sympathetically. "Those things happen all the time. No big deal at all. You learned something new today, that's all."

As the waitress turned to leave, Dagni's hand sprang up like a fountain.

"Uh, m'am," she called out, much louder than usual. "Uh, no rush or anything, but I think you forgot something—the coconut pie!"

Linda Marie Harris

"Do you want sugar, milk, or juicy gossip, with your tea?"

Sweet Violets

The mere chink of cups and saucers
turns the mind to happy repose.

George Gissie

"Battlefield tea, unaccompanied by typical ceremony, cleared his head, claimed the Duke of
Wellington to his staff at Waterloo.'" I read the
sentence aloud from a newspaper article on trivia.
"Battlefield tea," I mused and looked again at the solitary
cup and saucer squatting in my china hutch. "Maybe
that's what happened to the rest of your kin. Forfeited on
the field in the interest of war!"

I'd discovered the delicate pair in an out-of-the-way
antique store the prior summer. Lifting them from their
perch—perilously near the edge of a crowded discount
shelf—I examined them. Although a small stubborn stain
blotched the bottom of the cup's bowl, nary a nick or crack
marred the cup and saucer. I gave into my urge, made the
purchase, and brought them home.

After a time-tested vinegar soaking and some gentle
scrubbing, I managed to eliminate the stain. A graceful
dip of deep-hued violets swirled the rim and cheered me
each time I walked past them. When I needed a mind-

melting cuppa chamomile or a bracing swig of Earl Grey or a throat-soothing sip of honey ginseng, I found myself reaching for that lone little cup. We'd forged a relationship, the two of us.

So I began a search for the rest of the set. Hoping against hope, like all avid antiquers, to add a cup or two from here and a few saucers from over there, I haunted flea markets, tag sales, and auctions. Once, while vacationing on the Eastern seaboard, I was tempted to purchase a partial set that would have "blended" with my cup-o-violets. But I resisted.

Instead, I gave up the hunt, opting to only use the cup and saucer when I fixed a lonely tea-for-one.

Months later, I sat in the home of a new neighbor, a fellow antique aficionado. She served us tea in vintage cups . . . from the same pattern as mine!

Surely not! As unobtrusively as possible, I searched for differences. Variance in color. Deviations in size. Discrepancy in shape. I couldn't find any differences, any at all. So I had to ask. "This china, wherever did you find it?"

"Oh, at an estate sale. What a steal!" Her arm swept wide to indicate the hutch behind her. "See? I bought them all."

And I ogled what I'd failed to notice before: a luscious stack of violet glistening behind the bow-fronted glass door. I swear, my mouth watered at the sight.

I swallowed hard. I gulped some tea. My eyes narrowed. I forced a tight smile. "How fortunate for you."

"Not so fortunate," she shook her head in denial. "There's a cup and saucer missing. And I've searched high and low—antique stores, auctions, yard sales. I'm afraid it's hopeless."

With one finger, I traced the willowy handle of the cup sitting in front of me. I toyed with the matching saucer. I took a long, lingering sip. And I looked directly into her amiable eyes.

"Have I got a surprise for you!"

After all, I reasoned, I'd met my Waterloo. Besides, the Duke of Wellington was wrong. Tea was at its best served with ceremony. A drink shared—not on the battlefield, but between friends.

Carol McAdoo Rehme

Tea Time with Dad

Its liquor is like the sweetest
dew from heaven.

Lu Yu

D ad was the Rural Route Two mail carrier in my
hometown of Rock Falls, Illinois, for over thirty
years. Every morning, he'd get up at 5:00, go to
the post office, sort the mail, then pack it into his car
from which he'd deliver it to his 500 patrons scattered
up and down blacktop and gravel roads for more than
fifty miles.

Around nine o'clock each morning, Monday through
Saturday, Dad would stop at home for a quick breakfast
before heading out to deliver the mail. In the years when I
was still an only child, before my brother and sister were
born, Dad's morning ritual often included tea with me in
my bedroom.

I was only four, five, and six years old during those tea
parties, but I remember them clearly. First, the begging,
"Daddy, please, please come back to my room for a tea
party before you leave."

"Okay, I'll be back as soon as I finish having breakfast
with your mother."

I'd scurry off to my room to make the preparations. Mother had given me her childhood set of mint-green Depression Glass child's dishes—two cups, two saucers, two four-inch-diameter sandwich plates, a creamer, and a sugar bowl. No teapot. No problem. I'd already learned that pouring tea with a pretend teapot is not a problem as long as you have real cups to pour it into.

I'd scoot my desk chair into the middle of my bedroom for Dad, and I'd straddle the lower end of a combination wooden table/bookcase that Dad had made for my knick-knacks. The top part of that little table was the perfect place for the tea dishes.

After I poured the pretend tea, and set the pretend cakes and pretend tea sandwiches on the two sandwich plates, I'd pick up my tiny teacup and blow on it to cool the steaming pretend tea. Then I'd settle back and ask Dad a question.

"So, what's new, Daddy?"

We talked about our big family garden, and he would remind me to help Mom pick raspberries that morning. Sometimes we talked about my turtles out in "Pat's Turtle Ranch," the words he'd carved into the concrete he had poured around an old tractor tire as a home for my growing collection of live turtles.

On those tea-party mornings, Dad listened more than he talked as I prattled on about my best friend Vivian, who lived up the hill next door to us. Some mornings I hauled out my dress-up clothes and paraded around my room as a fancy dancing queen or an elegant lady for my dad's enjoyment.

Dad may have even brought the newspaper with him into my bedroom on a few occasions while we sipped pretend tea together. It doesn't matter what we talked about, did, or thought during those tea parties. What matters is that for fifteen minutes during his busy "Have to go to work now, honey" mornings, my dad took the time to have tea with his daughter. The tea wasn't real. The sandwiches, cookies, and cakes weren't real. But the love I felt from my dad sure was. And to this day, I still love a good tea party, with real tea, of course, especially when Dad's around to enjoy it with me.

Patricia Lorenz

Une Tasse de Thé

When one has tea and wine,
one will have many friends.

Chinese Proverb

After two weeks in France, I found myself counting the days till we would fly back to the States. Although I was enjoying my spring trip with my older son, Anthony, I was starting to miss my husband and younger son who had stayed back in California for work and school. Anthony indulged me throughout our trip by seeking out the nearest Internet café in each town we visited so I could stay in touch with my guys back home.

Upon our arrival in Aix-en-Provence, we found an Internet café that also happened to be the local watering hole. Every day, we stopped by the café and sat at separate computer terminals so we could check our e-mails and write to family and friends. One afternoon, after reading a romantic e-mail from my husband, I felt more homesick than ever. I wrote back, and then logged off the computer to tell Anthony I was ready to leave the smoke-filled café and go find some supper. I saw him at the bar drinking beer and conversing with another gentleman—in rapid-fire French.

Although I speak French, I could only understand the occasional word. Since there were no empty seats near my son, I found a spot at the end of the bar by the door with cleaner air and a view of the busy, cobblestoned street. The bartender, friendly and patient with my limited French, took my order.

"Une tasse de thé, s'il vous plaît?" I asked in broken French. He promptly served up a tiny pot of hot water and a cup with a tea bag. As he served me, he said something that sounded like, "Another lady orders tea. An American." I nodded and smiled, acting like I understood. I slowly sipped the fragrant brew, and he left to serve other patrons. Glancing out the door, I watched people scurrying up and down the street—couples and families out enjoying the late afternoon. How fun it would be to walk arm-in-arm with my husband down the old streets of Aix, past cafés and cathedrals, taking in the sights. I missed him. But instead of feeling homesick, I cupped my hand around the warm cup and tried to savor my tea.

The waning afternoon light turned into evening, and I felt the pensiveness brought on by "l'heure bleu." The bartender refilled the tiny cup with hot water, and as I tried to coax the tired tea bag back to life, I had an idea where the expression "down in the cups" had originated. With a sea of foreign voices all around and my son preoccupied with his new acquaintance, I had never felt so alone.

"Voilà!" The bartender spoke. I looked up from my tea to see the friendly face of a woman, about my age, with salt-and-pepper hair. It was the American he had spoken of earlier. She offered her hand and introduced herself as

Habiba. Along with her daughter, Habiba was living in Aix while doing some research at the local university. Although she had been born in Algeria, she had lived and worked in the States for many years and was currently living in Atlanta.

She ordered her tea and sat down next to me while her daughter used the Internet. We quickly settled into a comfortable conversation—in rapid-fire English—discussing our families, motherhood, the South, and everything else in between. The time passed quickly as I listened to her lilting Southern/French accent and felt suddenly very much at home in the fading twilight.

An hour or so later when it was time to leave, we exchanged e-mail addresses and promised to keep in touch. When I returned to the States, we e-mailed each other and deepened our friendship for the next several months. When she wrote to tell me she would be in California for the holidays, we decided to get together for brunch.

On the appointed day, the first thing I saw when she and her husband pulled up was her smiling face. She climbed out and we hugged, and I felt I had known her for years. She handed me a gift bag.

I can't say I was surprised with what I found inside the bag—a cheerful tin of designer tea bags—green tea with cherry blossoms. As our families visited and got to know each other further, Habiba and I picked up our conversation right where we'd left off at the Internet café in Provence. We spoke of work, children, health, and hopes. Soon, I told her, we were going to move to the Georgia countryside just a few hours north of her. Knowing such a wonderful, new friend would be nearby was a big comfort to me and gave me confidence about our upcoming move.

"I can't believe we had to travel halfway around the world to meet each other," Habiba said, squeezing my hand. Brought together by fate, I thought, or a simple cup of tea.

Janie Dempsey Watts

Origins of Tea

Asian countries, specifically China, India, and Sri Lanka, account for 80 percent of the tea grown in the world.

India exports more than 12 percent of the world's tea. Three of the largest Indian tea producers are

- Assam (from the Himalayas to the Bay of Bengal)

- Darjeeling (from the foothills of the Himalayas)

- Nilgeri (from southern India)

Sri Lanka (or Ceylon) tea accounts for 21 percent of the world's exports. Dimbrita (harvested 5,000 feet above sea level), Kenilworth, Uva, St. James, Nuwara Eluja, and Ceylon Blend are the most popular teas from Sri Lanka.

Africa is home to 15 percent of the tea-growing countries. Kenya actually rivals China in the volume of tea produced. Located on the equator, the majority of Kenya's tea fields are in the mountainous rainforest region.

A Cup of China Tea

In London, love and scandal are
considered the best sweeteners of tea.

John Osborne

Some places are etched in one's memory forever. One of mine is the London teahouse we visited many years ago. We made our way there on a gray, blustery day, ignoring the on-and-off drizzle. All the guidebooks said it was a must-see. Map in hand, my husband and I squinted at street signs, hurried across crowded intersections, and gratefully accepted directions from friendly passersby. Apparently, everyone knew the place. Its façade seemed right out of Dickens—multipaned windows, green awning flapping in the wind, old-fashioned lettering on a painted wooden sign in the shape of a teacup swinging above the narrow door. We found the inside equally charming as we felt its warmth easing the outside chill. Small tables were scattered about, covered with flowered cloths and pots of steaming tea. And, oh, the smells! Hot scones and spiced tea, clotted cream and chocolate. My mouth watered. As the guidebook suggested, we'd arrived unfashionably early, and we were in luck. A tall, elegant man who could pass for a butler greeted us and motioned to someone.

"Tourists, are you? Americans, I bet." The pert young waitress approached us with a lovely smile. She wore a gray uniform with a starched white apron and a small, triangular crown sitting on top of her dark curls. She was fascinated when she learned we were Californians. It was useless to insist we'd never met any film stars. She was clearly impressed with our celebrity. She told us her name was Milly, and she'd just turned eighteen. "I'd have the high tea," she suggested, her bright blue eyes glancing at the delicate-looking clock on the wall above. "Yes, it's just time." How could we resist cucumber sandwiches, savories and sweets, and heavenly pots of special tea?

She brought us our first course on a three-tiered china platter filled with small crustless sandwiches, shrimp paté, chopped egg, some kind of meat paste, and, of course, cucumber. Next came scones with pots of jam and cream. "The strawberry's the best," Milly whispered. *How did she keep that tiny waist if she tasted everything?* I wondered. Chimes on the front door tinkled, and, suddenly, the sunny expression on Milly's face turned to one of gloom as she noticed the new arrival. "Oh, no, not her. I just know Mr. Hastings is going to put her at one of my tables."

The woman at the door seemed hardly the type to provoke such anxiety. She was tiny, dressed in a somewhat dated tan tweed suit, with a brown wool shawl draped across her shoulders. Her eyes darted everywhere as she tucked a stray wisp of white hair back into her brown velvet hat. Mr. Hastings waved a hand; Milly heaved a sigh and hurried off.

The newcomer's voice sounded surprisingly robust for one with so small a frame. "No, I want the table over there, please." She pointed a black umbrella toward the wall near us. Millie turned toward the door, and I saw Mr. Hastings nod. The older woman pulled herself erect, oblivious to some patronizing stares following her. We heard a soft groan as she settled down in her chair and pulled off her leather gloves. "I'll have the scones with clotted cream and fresh strawberry jam—it is fresh?" Milly nodded her head. "And real China tea, mind you, it must be real China tea!"

My husband cautioned me not to stare, but I couldn't help myself. Something about her intrigued me. She had a mind of her own and a spunky presence that belied her age. The smile was gone from the young girl's face as she came over to refill our teacups and bring us a tray of tiny pastries. "She's always like that, and such a loud voice, too!"

"Perhaps she's hard of hearing," my husband offered. Milly just shrugged and turned away.

Always like that? We wondered how often she came here. I tried not to be too obvious as I watched her scones and tea arrive. Carefully, she took a sip. "This is not China tea!" she exclaimed.

"Oh, yes, Ma'am, it is," Milly said. "See, it's written right here."

The woman in tweed ignored the slip of paper. "I know China tea, young lady. My late husband, Arthur, and I always had China tea here—and this is not China tea!" I heard a muffled giggle from a table where two fashionably dressed young women sat. As Milly picked up the pot with a grim face, I was also sure it was not China tea.

When I saw the elderly lady looking at us, I thought she might be embarrassed by her outburst. But no, her face was musing. Did we remind her of herself and Arthur? This time I didn't try to hide my curiosity. I smiled faintly. She nodded, dabbing her cheek with her napkin. Was that a tear? A new pot of tea arrived. A fleeting smile brushed across her face as she savored the taste. "Now," she said, looking right at us, "*this* is real China tea!"

Milly brought our check. "I'd like to pay for hers, too," my husband said.

She seemed shocked. "Why would you want to do that?"

"Because it makes me feel good," my husband answered.

"Do you have a grandmother?" I tried to explain.

"Yes, Ma'am, but my gramma's dead." Her young face softened.

As we were leaving, Mr. Hastings touched my arm. Perhaps he had seen me staring. "They came here often," he said softly, "and always on their anniversary. They fancied that very table. Now, she comes alone."

Ilene Herman

Special Tea

A Proper Tea is much nicer
than a Very Nearly Tea, which is one
you forget about afterwards.

Winnie-the-Pooh

Aunt Gertrude was my mother's aunt, which made her my grandaunt. She was more than grand in my eyes.

She graduated from Cornell University in 1920, and then achieved success in her career as a chemist in a man's world. She taught Sunday school, headed missions boards, wrote poetry, and translated books into Braille for the blind. Aunt Gertrude was always dressed "to the nines," matching her hats and gloves with beautifully tailored suits and dresses. She refused to be considered a mere spinster. She preferred to call herself our "maiden aunt" instead.

During the 1950s, Mother, my sisters, and I would visit Aunt Gertrude in her neat little apartment, stay overnight, then join her on educational forays into the big city, visiting museums and landmarks. The first activity of each visit, however, was Aunt Gertrude's sumptuous tea.

As we rode up in the elevator, Mother would repeat her last-minute warnings: "No elbows on the table, sit up straight, and do not slurp your tea or chew with your mouth open. Napkin in your lap and say 'please' and 'thank you.' Behave like proper young ladies."

By the time we entered the apartment, we would be terrified, afraid we'd forget one of these rules and embarrass Mother. One look at Aunt Gertrude's smile and twinkling blue eyes, however, always relieved our fears.

"Good afternoon, ladies," she greeted us. Aunt Gertrude was tall, always stood straight with shoulders back, and confined her wispy salt-and-pepper hair in a bun. I never saw her without jewelry. While preparing tea, she donned an oversized apron to protect her dress.

The kettle boiled, and Mother helped Aunt Gertrude set the table. First, we placed the handmade lace tablecloth, then a centerpiece of fresh flowers, sparkling silverware, linen napkins, and bone china so fragile you could see through it. While they worked and talked in the sunny kitchen, we three girls stood, fascinated, before her teacup collection. It was displayed behind glass in a tall, mahogany breakfront in the living room.

This collection of cups and saucers was unique, each one chosen personally from a different country, province, or state. Among her other interests, Aunt Gertrude liked to travel. She visited family, friends, and missionaries throughout the world. In each foreign country, she bought three items: a native costume, a doll, and a cup-and-saucer set. Her china collection was huge. The cups and saucers were all numbered and recorded in Aunt

Gertrude's notebook. The cup-and-saucer notebook could answer all of our questions. So could Aunt Gertrude. For our special tea, we each selected a favorite cup and saucer from the collection.

I remember being served tiny egg sandwiches (with the crust trimmed off, of course), fresh fruit cup, miniature cream puffs, and petit fours. Aunt Gertrude poured our tea from a delicate china teapot. Although she had lots of cups and saucers, she used only one teapot. It was white, with pink apple blossoms spilling over the lid. It matched her set of china.

As we ate, Aunt Gertrude would share with us some history of the teacups we had chosen that day. "Do you know where that blue flowered cup came from? No? Well, I'll tell you. That one came from Manila, a city in the Philippines," she'd explain. "Cousin Leon bought it for me in a little teashop near the university where he taught in the late 1930s. Did you know he stayed to teach during the Japanese occupation of World War II?"

My aunt knew the history of every teacup.

By the mid-1960s, Aunt Gertrude had retired and moved back to Harrisburg to be near our family. A few years later, no longer able to keep her apartment as clean as she liked, Aunt Gertrude and I scrubbed, dusted, and visited together every Tuesday morning. Afterward, with the apartment shining to her satisfaction, she made lunch for just the two of us. We relaxed and talked about travel, family, and those special teacups. Once again, Aunt Gertrude poured our tea from the apple-blossom teapot. Then she'd ask, "Do you know where that mother-of-pearl cup came from? Well, I'll tell you . . ."

Although she died shortly afterward, Aunt Gertrude's special teas continue with my grandchildren. We choose the prettiest tablecloth, and set out gleaming silverware and the best china. We fill dishes with little sandwiches, fruit, and cookies. The napkins are made of paper, and elbows are sometimes on the table, but "please" and "thank you" are used often. Now I'm the one who pours the tea. The spout on the old apple-blossom teapot is nicked, and glue holds the handle to the lid, but it wouldn't be a "special tea" without that teapot.

As we serve the cookies, I can imagine Aunt Gertrude sitting with us, asking the children, "Do you know where that green and gold cup came from? Well, I'll tell you . . ."

Priscilla Gertrude Simmons

Tea-Party Parenting

Under certain circumstances,
there are few hours in life more agreeable
than the hour dedicated to the
ceremony known as afternoon tea.

Henry James

I couldn't really afford the teapot, but I couldn't really resist it, either: a glossy green frog with big, friendly eyes, a smiling baby froggy perched on its back, and pursed lips that poured tea into tiny lily-pad cups with froggy handles. I passed by the teapot several times as I followed my young daughters around the gourmet kitchen shop, warning them not to touch anything, before we went next door to the discount hair-cutting place. Each time the teapot called to me with promises of fantasy tea parties where we'd wear long strands of pearls, lacy dresses, and fancy hats, holding our pinkies delicately in the air.

I bought the teapot.

The next day, I hosted my first tea party. I snapped photos of my daughters wearing long strands of beads, Sunday dresses, and fancy hats, holding their pinkies delicately in the air. We ate chocolate-chip cookies and sipped warm peppermint tea. The girls loved it. What a treat to eat cookies before dinner! How special to drink tea like a grown-up! I loved it, too, but for entirely different reasons. I relished the uninterrupted conversation, the stillness in the late afternoon, and the civility. No one fussed or whined or complained about the size of her cookie, the temperature of the tea, or how much attention her sister was getting. We chatted about pets, ponies, the ultimate birthday party.

I hadn't bought a too-expensive froggy teapot; I'd bought parenting magic.

Sometimes I plan an after-school tea party on a snowy afternoon just because I feel like baking brownies and licking the bowl (without any help!). Usually, though, I throw a surprise tea party for a specific reason. Nothing restores harmony during a period of more-than-the-usual number of sibling spats like chamomile tea and oatmeal cookies. Somehow, holding a warm mug of tea soothes angry feelings. We start by talking about our days—good things that happened, and bad things that happened. We share stories and let our guard down in a way that doesn't feel like a lecture from Mom or Big Sister (or worse, annoying advice from Little Sister). And the good feelings last far beyond the tea party.

When one of my daughters is having trouble with friendships and frustrations with schoolwork, I will treat us to a pre-homework tea party. We start with the usual good things and bad things, and ease into the specific problems as we sip Cinnamon Spice tea and snack on scones. Soon, hurt feelings fade, smiles return, and even fractions (the clique or mathematical variety) don't seem insurmountable. The homework gets done. The friendship is restored.

Our tea parties provide a family support group, a safe place to talk, and sometimes they're a sneaky intervention. Recently, I discovered that my youngest daughter wasn't wearing her new glasses at school. She would wear them in the car and immediately after school, but not during class when she most needed them. Reasoning hadn't worked. Tearful talks with the teacher hadn't worked. Rewards hadn't worked. Punishment didn't matter. She hated her glasses and refused to wear them.

Time for a tea party.

I made vanilla tea and my daughter's favorite mini-molten chocolate cakes. While mixing the cake batter, I fretted about how to approach the topic of glasses. How do I convince a girl that she can overcome the decades-old smart-geeky-ugly-glasses-wearing stereotype? I feared this would be my first tearful tea party. But I was wrong. We talked about the things we liked about ourselves (hazel eyes, dark brown hair, imaginations), and things we wished we could change. My oldest wished she would never have to do math again. I talked about taming my feisty temper. My youngest looked at us and smiled. "You know," she said. And so we talked about vision and the consequences of poor vision (not seeing the stars at night, doing poorly in math, getting headaches). We discussed taking care of our health.

No one cried. We drank two pots of tea. Then we each vowed to do something personally difficult for ourselves.

🫖 Getting to the Heart of the Matter

Scientists believe that tea flavonoids (the antioxidant properties) help reduce the risk of cardiovascular disease, heart attacks, stroke, and high blood pressure.

One study showed tea consumption improves the function of the lining of the blood vessels. Arteries of regular tea drinkers have a better capacity for expansion and contraction. They also develop plaques and lesions associated with heart disease less often.

(I'm not sure how I'll make it through a week of not raising my voice.) I don't know if my youngest will ever love her glasses, but she knows it's important to all of us that she wear them. And she is willingly facing the challenge, thanks to a friendly tea party.

As my daughters grow older, I know that our tea parties will take on more serious topics. Thanks to my worth-every-dollar froggy teapot, we have our tradition of hot tea, freshly baked treats, and civility already in place. If the early stages of puberty are any indication, we are going to need it!

Sydney Salter Husseman

A "Teasmade" for Mum

I think of half-past four at Manderley,
and the table drawn before the library fire . . .
the performance, never-varying, of . . .
the silver tray, the kettle, the snowy cloth.

Daphne du Maurier

As far back as I can remember, I have started my day with a steaming hot cup of tea. It all began in the late 1920s when my mother awakened everyone in my family by saying, "Wake up, love. Your tea's ready," as she placed a steaming hot cup of tea on the chair next to the bed. The chair had two purposes: one, to set the tea on, the other to prevent us children from falling out of bed at night.

While in bed, I skillfully managed to drink my hot tea and stay snuggled under as much of the covers as possible. It didn't take long before the warm tea rushed through my body, giving me the courage to get out of bed on a cold, damp morning.

Our house in London, England, had a fireplace in every room. However, the only one with a roaring fire in the winter months was in the living room where, as a family, we spent our evenings. There were four girls and one boy, and Mum and Dad in our family. Mum was the only one of us who got out of bed each morning without the lovely feeling of being warmed by a cup of hot, freshly brewed tea. Dad made up for that on Sundays, and he included a muffin or cream cake, fresh from the bakery close by.

I expect it was this early introduction to tea that has made it so special for me. One time during World War II, our family fled from the air raids in London to an area that was safe from the falling bombs. We found refuge at the local Salvation Army center, and the first thing we were given was a cup of tea, which had a cheery, calming effect on all of us.

In 1949, I moved to America and settled in Wisconsin where my sister Connie was living with her GI husband. Many years later, I would regularly visit Connie, who was in a nursing home. Although Connie was slowly deteriorating because of Alzheimer's disease and no longer knew me, I found a cup of tea would temporarily work wonders for her memory. The mention of a few familiar places from Connie's childhood while she was having her cup of tea made her smile. As her frail hands wrapped themselves around the teacup filled with luke-warm tea, she would say to me, "I had the best mum and dad, didn't I?" I'm sure she was remembering her morning cup of tea as a child.

Years later while visiting London, I was in a department store when I spotted a colorful box on a shelf. In the box was a small, stainless-steel kettle with a tube that led into a china teapot. Once it was plugged in and its timer was set, it would awaken you with a hot pot of tea. The name of the item was "Teasmade." By this time, Mum and Dad's bedroom had an electric fireplace, but as I walked back to their house that day with the Teasmade under my arm, a tear ran down my face as I smiled and said to myself, *Now Mum can finally have a cup of tea before getting out of bed on a cold winter's day.*

Pearl Blanchett

🫖 Across the Pond

In the United Kingdom, only 30 percent of the tea drinkers take sugar, honey, or artificial sweetener in their tea.

However, 98 percent of the U.K. tea drinkers add a splash of milk.

Rescued by Joe and a Cuppa Tea

> The British have an umbilical cord
> which has never been cut and through
> which tea flows constantly.
>
> *Marlene Dietrich*

B y night, the empty street looked sinister with three- and four-story chipped brick buildings. A stillness pervaded the neighborhood. Only a weak, cold wind breathed across my face, causing me to shiver beside my backpack. I was sixty miles out of London in a dirty, industrial suburb named Luton—and desperate for a place to spend the night. A few minutes before, I had been deposited on the street by a lorry driver with whom I'd hitched a ride from the port.

I'd already gone one night without sleep. The cross-channel ferry trip from Belgium had offered the delights of a tossing sea. Several months into my round-the-world journey, tonight was now beginning to look like it would be just as long. Then, down the street, I noticed a white, round lamp on which was emblazoned the word "Police."

Hmmm. What safer place to be? The English bobbies were generally friendly fellows. Once inside the warm precinct house, I spoke to the young policeman behind the desk, explaining my predicament. He scratched his head, sympathetic to my plight, but due to recent terrorist attacks, nothing could be done. He did, however, offer me a cup of hot tea, which I gratefully accepted with a grin. It wouldn't happen in many American precincts. A few moments later, a wiry little guy with gray hair came in and chatted with the officers about his stolen car. The officer directed him over to the sofa where I sat. I noticed the man's gray and worn coat, and the creases on his weary face.

"Have a car stolen?" I asked him, out of the American sense of politeness.

"Yeah," he replied, "but turned out to be my best mate just borrowin' it." The accent was Scottish. I asked him if the police had found the car, and he waved his hand in a motion of dismissal. "These clowns couldn't catch a cold." I laughed.

"American?" he asked.

"Yeah," I replied, giving a brief synopsis of my latest travel crisis.

"I'm Joe," he said, introducing himself. Before he could say more, the officer called him back to the counter and said a few quiet words to him about his car. While Joe signed something and handed the paper to the officer, he gestured to me and said, "I'll take him home with me." It was stated matter-of-factly, like there had been nothing to think over. I offered a humble "thanks," reasoning that if Joe were a murderer, he'd hardly have offered me a place to stay in front of a policeman.

We drove to his apartment building. Inside, a fire blazed in a stone hearth, and a German shepherd lay comfortably near a sofa. The room was compact, but cozy. A long, narrow kitchen extended off the living room, and in it, a slim woman in her forties stood at a counter. I felt instantly at home.

"Brought us a guest home," Joe called out amiably. The woman came out and shook my hand warmly. "I'm Frances," she said with a smile. "Why don't you make yourself comfortable there on the sofa next to the fire? I'll go prepare three nice cups of tea."

I was telling Joe about my backpacking trip around Europe when Frances brought in a tray laden with a teapot, cups, and saucers, and a tiny milk jug, all of which felt so English.

We chatted through a third cup of tea before Joe had the idea to visit the neighborhood pub. "A good Scottish pub it is!" he said emphatically.

After donning sweaters and coats, we stepped back out into the damp and chilly air. The three of us crossed the street and walked about a block before entering The Glasgow Arms—a lively pub filled with folks who reminded me of the villagers in the movie, *How Green Was My Valley*. They were simple, hard-working souls, dressed plainly and poorly, who, despite hard economic times, were chatting, joking, and laughing. The austerity of this pub bordered on the extreme. The walls were naked, and only a row of dark bottles and clear glass mugs lined the shelves. In the background, a jukebox was belting out an American sixties' song, but the music was fighting a losing battle to the raucous crowd.

Joe, Frances, and I found a table in the middle of the room and sat down. At the table next to us, a large man in his fifties, gray-haired and red-faced, guzzled no less than two mugs of beer in the time it took for me to finish my story. The guy's three buddies, equally huge, guffawed merrily while quaffing beers.

"That's Eddie," said Joe, noting my interest in the big drinker. "It's his birthday today." He called out a greeting to Eddie, which I doubt Eddie was capable of hearing, due to both the noise and his level of consciousness. Suddenly, big Eddie keeled over and hit the floor with a loud crash. There was a smattering of applause and laughter as his buddies quickly pulled him upright and set him back in his chair. He sat immobile in the chair, smiling dumbly. His friends, as well as Frances and Joe, chuckled.

"Yeah," said Joe, "big Eddie turned fifty today. This is his big celebration!" I wondered how Eddie would feel the next day about being fifty. When the barmaid brought him over a rather large mug of hot tea, I laughed.

Some more of the evening slipped away, and we departed the pub, penetrating one of those dreamed-of English mists to return home. Once there, Joe showed me my room, more luxurious than I had expected. I would have been thrilled with the living-room sofa. The double bed was piled high with heavy blankets, and a dark oak wardrobe and a tiny lamp at my bedside accentuated the hominess of the room. After saying good night to my hosts, I climbed into bed and scribbled some notes in my journal. It didn't take long to fall into a wonderful, deep sleep.

Early in the morning, there was a knock at the door. Joe cheerfully bade me a good morning while carrying in a tray with a mug of steaming hot tea on it.

"C'mon down whenever you're ready," he told me, setting the tray beside the bed. He left to finish getting ready for work, and I sipped my tea, grateful for the fresh-tasting cream and sweet sugar. Only in England does tea have quite this good a taste! Afterward, immersing my soul in the brew, I got up, dressed, and went downstairs.

Frances was in the kitchen cooking breakfast. The smell of sizzling bacon permeated the house, its crackling a welcome sound to my stomach. Standing at the ready was yet another pot of tea. Joe stood in the living room pulling on his boots and coat. When I thanked him profusely for his rescue and hospitality, he said, "You're welcome anytime." After shaking hands, he departed for a day of labor. Sitting in a deep-cushioned chair in the living room, I feasted on an ample meal of toast, bacon, eggs, sausage, and more tea. I ate with relish. Within the hour, I was adjusting the straps on my backpack. Standing on Frances and Joe's doorstep, facing a gray but beautiful day, I shook hands with Frances.

"Now you drop us a line soon, and come back to visit when you come through Luton again." The smile on her tired face was genuine. I had no doubt as to who would inherit the kingdom of heaven.

Scott Sutton

cancer-Fighting Properties of Tea

Both black and green teas contain antioxidants that have cancer-fighting benefits.

Scientists from California and China completed a study that showed tea drinkers were about half as likely to develop stomach or esophageal cancer as non-tea drinkers.

A seventeen-year study in Sweden found that women who drink one cup of tea a day cut their risk of developing ovarian cancer by 24 percent, and those who drank two cups of tea a day lowered their risk by 46 percent.

Scientists in the United States have discovered that green tea may also be able to prevent skin cancer, and scientists in Spain and England have actually used the antioxidants to shrink cancer cells in animals.

The anti-cancer health benefit of green tea seems to be dose-dependent. An adult needs two bottles of concentrated green tea a day, providing the same antioxidants as sixty-eight bottles of Snapple or 112 bottles of SoBe green tea.

The concentrate seems to be the only practical source for providing anti-cancer health benefits, since other studies indicate that overdosing on green tea can also be harmful.

Nonna's Big Tea-Party Flop

*The tea party supposes neither
appetite nor thirst, and has no object
but distraction, no basis but
delicate enjoyment.*

Jean-Anthelme Brillat-Savarin

I t was the forties, and my grandmother, Nonna—
Angela Irene Giani DeBernardi, a fine artist with a
degree from a university in Florence, Italy—was
going to give a tea party. She spoke four languages and
hiked the Alps with painting paraphernalia on her back.
Nonna. An elegant woman who married the widower of
her sister, becoming mother to my mother and uncle, and
leaving behind her wealthy family. Nonna. Rich no more.
An immigrant lumped into a stereotype that blanketed
Italians.

"I would like to invite you to come to my tea party and
help," she said one fine spring day, holding a brush
between her teeth, squinting at some section of a work in
progress. I thought I was going to faint at the idea of being
included in such a grown-up event.

Several months back, the family men had returned from
the Connecticut State Fair with a little organ-grinder mon-

key we named "Chico." Nonno, my grandfather, had won him by singing a German song, no less. Truth be told, since Nonno's voice was terrible, the women were certain Chico's previous owners would have done anything to get rid of him. For eight months, the little devil lived loosely with all our families and caused so much havoc in the town that he even made the newspapers. When Nonna decided to have a tea party for the neighborhood ladies, she certainly had no intention of inviting Chico.

We began preparations. I delivered twenty-four hand-painted invitations, each with a different wildflower, done in the exquisite calligraphy Nonna learned as a girl. My *Zias* (Aunts), Mimi and Irma, scrubbed the house from top to bottom because it was well known that Nonna was an artist, not a housekeeper. I helped shine little silver spoons for the chocolate, tea, and espresso sets. Delicate as a bird's egg, the cups were hand-painted with periwinkle blue and butterscotch glazes. Fine ivory linen napkins, crafted by Nonna's sister—the grandmother I never knew—were washed, starched, and ironed.

The day of the huge event, my shortened mop was curled around my head, styled expertly by Roberta Pellegrini. I'd miraculously survived the bath ordeal where I was scrubbed raw. Mamma tugged lace-edged socks over my feet and buckled on brand-new white Buster Browns. Then came the washed, starched, and ironed best dress: the white eyelet, with a long baby-blue satin ribbon drawn through a high waist and tied in a neat back bow. Finally came a squirt of Mamma's best perfume and snow-white gloves.

"Turn," she ordered. A smile touched her whole face as she marched me out our back door. "La bella!" she trumpeted to Nonna, giving my cheeks one last violent pinching.

Nonna's dress was a pleated and pressed navy silk, topped with her best handmade white-lace collar. She was wearing her huge, smoky pearl earrings, a little lapel watch Mamma had bought her with "faux" diamonds, and a double strand of pastel coral beads from the old country.

"You stand tall, my beautiful granddaughter," Nonna commanded, while moisture touched her eyes. "You come from elegant people. Show it."

I stretched up high and squared off my shoulders, smiling broadly at Nonna, filled to the brim with everything.

The ladies began to arrive. Dressed in their best, speaking polite hellos in a dozen different accents, they offered gloved hands. Family jewelry that had also survived the long journeys to this new country was displayed from ample bosoms, pink ears, slim or wattled necks, wrists, and fingers. Every piece had a story; every story defined a person. Corsets were drawn tight. Girdles girdled. Mouths and nails were painted ruby wine.

Nonna and I greeted each guest at the front door with warm smiles. I showed everyone to the parlor, and took wraps and purses. Nonna began to take orders for chocolate, tea, or coffee. I helped, holding each cup with a napkin underneath, delivering it to the smiling faces. Next came the jellyroll cakes and the buttery, almond sugar cookies, all adorning the delicate plates, rimmed with gold and sprinkled with pink flowers. I sat politely on the ottoman, and was just about to take my first bite when Chico made his grand entrance, flying through the open dining-room window.

One woman screamed and jumped up, while her lap-ful of sweets clattered to the floor. Eleven others fol-lowed suit. Cakes, coffee, tea, chocolate, and espresso spilled down bosoms, onto laps, and over the carpet. Nonna captured the little bag of trouble, embraced the stunned monkey in a bear hug, ran out the kitchen door, knocked over my little brother David, and raced to the chicken coop.

Unceremoniously, she threw Chico in with the biddies, slammed everything shut, and sprinted back up the hill, holding up her navy dress. You could hear wing-flapping and hysteric clucking from the hens who'd been suddenly incarcerated with a fiend.

Inside, the women were picking up their hats, brushing cake off the floor, and mopping up the spills on their dresses, chairs, and rug with hankies, and bath and kitchen towels.

"It was only Chico," I stammered, trying to explain. "Nonno puts sweets out, and he comes for them."

The women laughed nervously, while Nonna tried to get them to sit, offering more sweets and drinks. They declined and soon went home, one by one, offering polite excuses that were not the truth. Nonna didn't tell me what to do when people left, so I just stood on the sun porch repeating, "It was only Chico."

When the last guest departed, we went to the kitchen, and Nonna collapsed into a chair. She put her two hands

over her heart like all the pictures of the saints at St. Mary's
Catholic Church, rolled suffering eyes heavenward,
moaned "Dio," and assumed the persona of the suffering
and completely mortified tea-party Virgin Mary.

"Your Nonna, she is a big tea-party flop."

"No, you're not!" I retorted in a huff. "They shouldn't be
scared of a little monkey, for gosh sakes!"

David had edged halfway into the kitchen and stood
hanging on the door jam.

"Chico scared all the ladies," I explained, holding a delicate demitasse in my still gloved, but smudged hand.
"And all the women started screaming. Then they left. It
was only Chico, for gosh sakes."

Behind him came Mamma, and my zias. They just went
in the parlor and started cleaning the mess.

"Nonna thinks she's a big flop," I howled to everybody,
who were silently carting all the breakage and leftover
sweets to the kitchen sink.

"That darn cretin monkey," hissed Mamma, washing
some surviving cups. "This is getting ridiculous, let me tell
you. The whole box of expensive chocolates I bought is
scattered to the walls!"

My brother shot for the living room.

The rest of the afternoon we had the best tea party.
There wasn't too much damage to the china, which was
a miracle. For weeks, Nonna's oriental carpet smelled like
vanilla and chocolate instead of Nonno's cigars. The
more we talked about things, the more we laughed. And
when the men got home, the laughter started all over.
The only thing we had for supper was dessert. We were

all completely over the edge when somebody remembered Chico in the chicken coop. He had been making himself at home up on a high roost, cozying up to a big biddy. I could see it in his eyes. That monkey was thinking and planning more devilish mischief.

They're all gone now, except David and me. Every day, I pass the framed napkins in my bedroom and remember that in the long years since that day, there has never been anything that could match the uninvited guest, the utter chaos he created, and our family, who took total failure and turned it into a hilarious free-for-all tea, with spoonfuls of love.

Isabel Bearman Bucher

Time for Raspberry Tea

There is no trouble so great or grave
that cannot be much diminished
by a nice cup of tea.

Bernard-Paul Heroux

I was never really a tea drinker. I dabbled. A cup here. A cup there. Not even sure what kind it was.

Then one day, my friend Joan and I wandered into the local health-food store for lunch. Tuna salad and chicken salad topped with bean sprouts and sesame seeds were our sandwiches of choice. For dessert? Raspberry tea from a box she pulled off the shelf while we were waiting in line to pay our bill.

"Why raspberry?" I asked.

"Because I want to try something new," she replied. "I take several tea breaks throughout the day, and I haven't tried this kind yet. We'll go to my house and have a cup of tea."

"I don't really drink tea," I sheepishly replied. "But it sounds like a great idea anyway."

Once inside those welcoming walls of home, it was seconds before the hot water was sending out its steaming message: "It's tea time."

"We're going to use the good cups," Joan said, as she placed beautiful pink-and-white flowered cups on matching saucers.

We each took a tea bag from the newly purchased box and placed them gingerly into our cups. When the boiling water hit the tea bag, an explosion of light-pink liquid turned into a full-bodied raspberry rhapsody within minutes. The aroma of crimson-colored leaves filled the kitchen with its music.

Just maybe there's something to this tea thing after all, I thought.

Juggling our fancy cups of raspberry-flavored delight, we each took our favorite chair in the living room. I always sat in the chair under the winter scene painted by a family friend. And Joan sat in hers, the one closest to the front door . . . the same front door I came through as a teenager almost fifty years ago. If those two chairs could talk, they would reveal five decades of friendship.

As the memories and the tea met my lips, I began to cry. "I miss my mother," I whispered into my teacup. I was going through a difficult time. I had just lost my mom at the age of ninety-three to that brazen thief that tiptoed into her life and shamelessly robbed her of her memory.

Mom's last few years were filled with confusion and anxiety. She left behind many children, grandchildren, and great-grandchildren. In the end, she knew some of us by name, but others she didn't. The Alzheimer's bandit didn't care if she had children or not, let alone if she remembered their names.

Those terrible images of Mom's illness crept into my mind. How does anyone forget to eat? How does anyone forget where the bathroom is? How does anyone forget you were just there when you step out of the room for a second?

In happier times, when I used to visit Mom, she always had a fresh pot of coffee brewing on the stove. Occasionally, we'd have an espresso or cappuccino to celebrate our day. I would fill her big brown mug with the word "Mom" etched on it, and then get myself the one with the brightly colored Christmas tree painted on it. No matter what time of the year it was, I loved the feeling of Christmas in my hands. It seemed to offer so much promise.

And now, as Joan and I sat talking for a long time, I sipped my tea as those painful images of my mother dissolved, making way for happier ones.

When I left the comfort of that room to go home, I took all the pain and beauty of those moments with me. My tears had dried, and my heart was full. The warm, fuzzy feeling from sharing my mom's life with a good friend over a cup of tea made me promise myself a trip to the tea aisle of the supermarket.

As I made my way to the shelves that harbored many varieties of tea, I shuffled through boxes of Lemon Zinger, Peach Passion, Mint Medley, Cranberry Apple, Ginger Twist, and Tangerine Orange in search of a very-much-wanted box of raspberry. Locating the prized box amidst all these aromatic sensations, I put it in the top section of my cart so nothing would squish it.

I have visited that chair, the one under the winter scene, time and time again. And it has always had a cup of raspberry tea on the table next to it. I can hear the clink of Joan's cup hitting the pink-and-white flowered saucer as she sits in the seat closest to the front door. More tears. More laughter. More sharing.

On many mornings now, I make myself a cup of raspberry tea, as I sit in my favorite chair in my own living room. Knowing I have so much to live for before God calls me home, I sip my tea in the cup that has "Mom" etched on it in bold brown letters and welcome its comfort. One cup at a time. One memory at a time. One day at a time.

🫖 Let Loose

If you're filling a tea ball or infuser with loose tea, fill it only halfway full. Tea leaves need space to expand as they steep. Most teas will more than double their size during steeping.

Better yet, put the loose tea directly into the pot and strain it when you pour it into the cups. That way the leaves will have plenty of room to rock and roll, steep, swirl, and swish in the water.

Lola Di Giulio De Maci

Dad's First Date

Where there's tea, there's hope.

Sir Arthur Pinero

My father, William George Williams, nursed my mother through a long illness before she passed away at fifty-eight years of age. Dad was sixty-two at the time of her death. After a sincere and difficult mourning period lasting six months, Dad made his first hesitant steps toward getting out into the social world once again.

As his only daughter, I thoroughly agreed with his decision. I was busy with my own life and didn't want to see Dad spending so much time alone. When he casually mentioned one day that a lovely widow at church had invited us both over to her home for tea, I couldn't help smiling. The idea seemed perfect as an icebreaker. It sounded "safe," since I'd be there to accompany him. My presence would make it seem like it wasn't really a date. This was simply the case of a fellow parishioner at church reaching out to two people who had suffered a family loss.

"I think it would be nice if you went, too," Dad suggested, his voice tight. He fidgeted nervously, and his expression appeared vulnerable as he waited for my response.

I sensed that Dad really wanted me to go, that my being there would make him feel more comfortable. I figured I could smooth over the conversation if it faltered.

"I've always wanted to see June's place," I said brightly, agreeing to accompany him the following Sunday afternoon. I approved of June's overture—not that it was my decision to make, of course. It also tickled my fancy that I, at age thirty-four, would function as a kind of chaperone and safety valve for my own Dad's jump back into the dating game.

I only hoped that this invitation to tea would serve its purpose. Hopefully, it would bring together in a safe and relaxed setting two people who were searching for companionship.

June was an attractive, well-dressed, soft-spoken widow that both my parents had known from their work on various church committees. I myself had heard only positive comments about June. One evening, after Mom had passed on, June and Dad found themselves sitting across the table from one another at a church dinner. This gave them the opportunity to gauge each other's personality. Something apparently clicked between them, and they decided to pursue a friendship.

I needn't have worried about how the afternoon would go. There was nothing strained about that get-together. June greeted us warmly at her door, pressing our hands in greeting. Then she hugged me and exclaimed how happy she was to see me. I have no idea if she hugged Father or not because I was already walking through the doorway into her immaculately kept stone house. June gave us a thorough tour, pointing out the many curios she'd brought back from vacations abroad.

We sat down in her spacious dining room where she served us Earl Grey tea, brewed in a silver teapot. "This is my mother's hand-painted china," she explained. "Mother painted this set as part of her hope chest for her wedding day." The delicate cups and saucers with their pastel swirls of color were a true work of art.

"That's wonderful," I commented, "that you still have this china as a memento of your mom." I was enchanted with the miniature sugar bowl with its tiny gold spoon.

We snacked on finger sandwiches and discussed the history of our community. June had lived in the borough longer than we had and updated us on many interesting details that we never knew.

After a pleasant hour or so, I took June up on her suggestion to check out her garden. That gave the two of them time to chat alone, which led to Father asking her out on a real date.

After a fun courtship, they were married a year later. Both are gone now, but good memories of these special people remain. Their lives are an example of how happiness, once lost, can always be regained.

Cheryl E. Williams

communicating Through the cup

Make tea, not war.

Author Unknown

"I thought you said they spoke some English," my husband whispered as we helped the three women, who were principals of schools in Afghanistan, carry their suitcases to their room in our home.

"I'm sure they speak some. It will be all right," I assured him quickly, not sure if it was the truth. We had hosted participants of the Afghan Teacher Exchange Program before, but they were English teachers, and they had spoiled us with their fluency. We had only learned a few words in Farsi, one of the languages these women spoke.

Many of these women educators had sown seeds of hope during the Taliban's reign by secretly holding school for both girls and boys in their homes. If they were caught, they and members of their families risked imprisonment or death. After the American-led forces freed the Afghan people from the Taliban, schools filled beyond their capacities. If their country was going to make the most of their newfound freedom, its children needed to be educated, they said.

The Afghan Teacher Exchange Program was established by the U.S. State Department and the University of Nebraska at Omaha International Studies Department to provide intense training for these educational pioneers. Most of the women had never left their families or traveled alone. I worried about them as their busy schedule of classes and activities left them exhausted.

Every morning I prepared each of them a cup of tea and placed *naan* (bread) on the table. Afghans use their tea to greet and say good-bye—and everything else that falls in between. They had shared their tea with me, and I had purchased a variety for them to try. They would linger as long as they could before we had to race out the door. Holding that teacup and sipping that familiar beverage seemed to renew them, making them ready for another day.

Somehow, we muddled through the first weeks. They did know some English, and we started learning Farsi. When our conversations reached a lingual impasse, Kaamila, one of the principals, would begin laughing and say, "Confused." We could often resolve the confusion by consulting one of their bilingual instructors the next school day.

One night, Kaamila received a phone call from home. When she returned the phone to the cradle in the kitchen, I saw her tear-stained cheeks. "Oh, Kaamila, what's wrong?" She started to sob, speaking in Farsi, trying to tell me of the news from home. I didn't understand. There were too many words I didn't know. I draped my arm around her and helped her back to her room. The other women saw her distress, and their arms replaced mine. I felt so completely helpless. Words. I was tired of words. How could I show her that I wished her peace when so much could not be said?

I returned to the kitchen and began unloading the dishwasher. The dishes were still warm. I cradled a teacup in my hand. Its heat felt good. And then I knew I could send that kind of reassuring warmth all the way to Kaamila's heart. I filled the cup with water and placed it in the microwave. After the timer beeped, I bobbed the tea bag into the hot water. Curls of golden brown seeped from the bag, changing the water's color. I carried the cup of tea to her room and handed it to her. "Tashacor," she said softly as I left.

The next evening after we cleared the dinner table, Kaamila began preparing some tea. When the water was ready, she asked me to join the three of them at the table. She bobbed a tea bag in her cup and then passed the cup to me. She pulled a piece of paper from her notebook and began to read: "My dear sister, thank you for your kindness. My father is very sick with a stroke. Thank you for the tea. I am glad to be in your house."

She folded the paper and put it back in her notebook. "Tashacor," I said, taking the fourth cup from the center of the table to pass to Kaamila. We enjoyed our tea without another word that evening, savoring a warmth that comes from being with friends of the heart.

Elizabeth Wells

Come for Tea

Top off the tea . . . it lubricates
the gray matter.

Paul Eddington
as Jerry Ledbetter, "Good Neighbors"

Rosie clipped the twisted brown twine holding the box, folded back the flaps, and lifted the card lying atop the tissue-paper packing. A stylized hand-drawn rose adorned the note card.

The package arrived in the morning mail, and she had left it on the bench by the door, glancing at it throughout the day as she went about her chores. She hadn't heard from that side of the family for years and wasn't sure she wanted to know what was in the box. Since Grandma Rosa Jane died, the family just hadn't kept in touch, and now, this package.

Flipping open the card, she recognized the note at the top—"Come for tea," written in her grandmother's distinctive hand. She remembered the cards, her grandma drawing each rose in pen, and she and Janie coloring them with colored pencils from Grandma's well-worn art box. Below was written, "We were cleaning out the attic at Grandma Rosa Jane's, and I knew you would want this.

Do you remember? Love, Janie."

Rosie lifted the crinkled, yellowing tissue, and there it was—the tea party.

They had tea together every Saturday afternoon during the cold winter months—Rosie, Janie, and Grandma. She lifted the teapot, examining the miniature roses in its pattern. She placed it, the creamer and sugar bowl, the two cups and saucers on her shining marble countertop. The antique tea set, with its old-fashioned pattern and cracked glaze, looked out of place in her modern apartment. She balanced firmly on the chrome bar stool, fingering the card. She could almost see the tea tray set for tea on the mahogany table near the fireplace in Grandma's parlor. She thought for a moment she could hear the fire crackling and Grandma saying, "Miss Janie, Miss Rosie, it's tea time."

She was about to discard the box when she saw the small bundle of cards tied with faded pink ribbon peeking from beneath the tissue paper—the cards lovingly made by her grandmother while entertaining her granddaughters. The girls would chatter away until the tea was ready and the tray was set with lemon cookies and white linen napkins. What a divine time they had each Saturday, rummaging through the trunks in the attic, and then having chamomile tea with Grandma Rosa Jane.

Rosie prepared a pot of tea and moved the tea set to the table by her favorite chair. Still holding the precious cards in her hand, she picked up the phone and dialed.

"Janie, can you come for tea?" A smile beamed across her face, and she could feel the warmth of her cousin's smile come through in her reply.

"Of course, I have my cup right here. It has been too long since we've had tea."

They chatted the afternoon away, remembering their childhood and catching up with their lives now. Rosie realized what she had been missing. The childhood connection to family was still there for her as an adult. She knew now what her grandmother knew all along—it just takes a little effort.

"Janie, I remember what Grandma always said. The tea is good, it warms your body, but it's the company and conversation at tea time that warms the soul."

Anita Machek

A Cup of Comfort

As long as it's hot and wet and goes down
the right way, that's all that matters.

The Duchess of York, on tea

M oving to a new city and state was difficult for my family, especially in winter. Little did we know that a Colorado blizzard would greet us after we had been in our new home for only a week. The excitement of a new adventure was dulled by the memories of the California sunshine and the five-foot snow banks outside our door. My husband and son took a more positive attitude than me, playing in the snow and taking pictures to send our family.

I just missed home. But more than our old house, more than the beach, and more than the seventy-degree warm weather, I missed Stacey. My best friend and I had both cried when I left, like two junior-high girls, not women in their forties.

"We will write and e-mail often," she promised.

"We'll visit, too. It's not like I'm moving to China," I added.

My computer became a dear friend to me the first months in Colorado. Opening up e-mail and finding a short note or a long letter from Stacey fought the loneliness and stress of change I felt each day. But I still missed her presence. I missed her reactions to my stories and the compassion in her face when I spilled my problems.

And I missed our lovely teas. Going to a sweet little tea room we had discovered was a special treat for us. The place was a Victorian dream, with delicate teacups and tablecloths with flower prints. The hat rack near the front swept us back to childhood. Stacey and I became little girls, trying on different hats until we found the perfect one for our dress-up tea party. We would then be escorted to a lovely table and order our tea. Those afternoon teas were precious times, filled with laughter between scones and sharing our lives between tiny cucumber sandwiches.

Springtime descended upon Denver, and the sun lightened my heart. But I still fought loneliness almost every day. I decided to become proactive and set about the adventure of exploring the Denver area. While my son went to school and my husband went to the office, I took time to see what our new area had to offer.

One day, I was driving to find a movie theater. A map of the streets of Denver was opened in the front passenger seat, but was not helping me much. I kept flipping its pages, hoping to miraculously find a message that read, "You are here: go here," with arrows pointing the way. I felt directionally challenged, frustrated, and confused. Tears came to my eyes, and I decided just to pull the car over and cry a while.

As I sat there sobbing, hoping no one driving or walking by would stare at the crazy, bawling woman in the car, my eyes scanned the buildings on the street. "Tea Leaves" caught my eye. A tea room? Here, in the land of loneliness and pain?

I wiped my eyes and got out of the car. A nice cup of hot Earl Grey would help.

I walked through the doors, and tears came to my eyes again. It was a beautiful room, not Victorian, but simple and lovely.

Stacey would love this place, I thought.

At the counter, a plump woman with a red face and an easy smile welcomed me.

"What can I get you?"

"Do you have scones?" I asked.

"Absolutely." Her smile warmed me, and I couldn't help but grin.

"My friend and I used to have tea in California at a tea room. I just loved the experience."

"Would you like to have a full tea?"

"You do that, too?"

"Of course."

I sat down and ordered a pot of tea, a cucumber sandwich, and some scones with Devonshire cream and English jam. It felt silly and wonderful—and it felt like home. For the first time since moving, I felt as if this new city and state could be, would eventually be, my home. Laughter came as I sat and ate the delicious food, and sipped the rosehip and hibiscus tea. I would come back here and bring new friends. I would sit and drink and write and enjoy the simple pleasure of being a wife and mom and woman. And when Stacey visited, we would come here and laugh and celebrate a friendship that will last beyond years and miles.

I lifted my cup and looked around to see that no one saw my silly gesture. Then I made a silent toast. I toasted Stacey, whom I missed dearly, and I toasted a sweet little tea room that lessened my pain.

Robbie Iobst

Feeling a Bit Pekoed?

Pekoe refers to the leaf size—small. It is thought that the original orange pekoe tea from China was flavored with orange blossoms, but these days orange pekoe generally refers to black tea made from small leaves.

Orange pekoe varies greatly in flavor, depending on the origin of the tea leaves and the processing. It is one of the most common teas.

Tea drinkers who enjoy a hearty, smoky, rich tea should try Lapsang Souchong. This tea, originally from China, is made from very large tea leaves. In fact, Souchong means "large leaves."

Phil Simms,
C. S. Lewis, and Tea

Real men drink tea!

Sting

I balked when I saw the ad in *Sports Illustrated*. Two blond, buffed men holding innocuous white cups with little tea labels slipping out from under the lids. The caption read, "Look Who's Drinking Bigelow Green Tea Now." The endorsement wasn't from just any cute athletes, but from two-time Super Bowl winner Phil Simms and his son, Tampa Bay quarterback Chris Simms. A sentence printed in the actual color of green tea directed me to a website.

I tried to imagine my husband and his buddies sporting grande-sized cups of green tea while they watched the Super Bowl.

"Hey, buddy," one would yell, "toss me one of them scones." A perfect lateral—score!

"Dude. Gimme a cute little cream-cheese sandwich."

Nope. Can't picture it. Not even with a celebrity endorsement.

I drink a lot of tea—usually two quarts per day. I never

met a tea I didn't like. Black, green, red, white—they all are precious in my sight. I like hot tea on cool days and iced tea on warm days. I never leave home without it.

I began to love tea in college when I spent a month in merry old England. While staying at Westminster School in London, the staff served hot tea for breakfast. Tried it. Loved it. Never quit.

Several of my friends live overseas, and they testify to tea's prominence as the world's favorite drink. In different areas of the globe, tea is ascribed medicinal properties. In parts of Russia, they say drinking green tea in the winter will ward off colds. In parts of China, the pharmacist may hand you a packet of specially blended tea leaves along with your Western prescription. Phil Simms says he drinks tea for "diet, nutrition, and a healthy lifestyle." Health, schmealth. I'd drink tea if it made me ugly, sick, and fat.

I use a kettle that belonged to my grandmother. It was one of her wedding gifts in 1937. The kettle is stainless steel and looks every bit of its seventy years. Still, it whistles on perfect pitch. I own other kettles, but they don't whistle for me. Flattery goes a long way.

My tea drawer usually contains three different flavors at any given time. You can tell the state of my finances by the quality of my tea. Living lean means Lipton. Ordinary time means Tazo, Republic of Tea, and Bigelow. When the rivers of abundance run free, I indulge in quality loose tea. Unfortunately, I have to drive seventy-five miles to purchase it, or buy online.

If you have never wandered into a tea emporium, try it. The variety of scents and colors gets my mouth watering before I even get a sip to my lips. I don't understand people who say, "I don't like tea," or "All tea tastes the same." Darjeeling tastes nothing like jasmine. There are teas for people who love caffeine and for people who avoid it. I imagine there are as many varieties of tea as there are people who drink it, with new creations brewing all the time.

🫖 Get Fit

Japanese researchers have found that drinking green tea before you exercise may improve your endurance by 24 percent. Green tea extract improves endurance by stimulating fatty acids that the body then uses as an energy source.

Scientists in Geneva, Switzerland, have discovered that the antioxidants called "catechin polyphenols" found in green tea help burn calories faster by jump-starting your metabolism.

At times, I am a tea purist, and at times I am not. I drink my tea straight—no milk, no sweeteners. George Orwell would be proud. In an essay about tea for the *Evening Standard* in 1946, he wrote, "Tea is meant to be bitter, just as beer is meant to be bitter."

Our taste buds that detect bitter flavors strengthen as we age; I suppose that is why I like my tea stronger as the years pass.

However, I will admit that on a 100-degree day, I have iced down even fine tea. I also (gasp!) sometimes drop green tea bags into cold water and let them sit overnight. When I travel, I use those hotel-room coffee makers to provide a nice warm cup of any available tea bag.

A benefit of my love of tea is that I am easy to buy gifts for. This year, my mother bought me a tea T-shirt, a tea calendar, a tea recipe book, a tea drip catcher for my teapot, and some quality loose tea—C. S. Lewis Tea Blend.

The label reads "Irish Breakfast tea blend, bold black tea from India's Assam region. Steep for 3–5 minutes in boiling water. Goes well with a book."

"You can never get a cup of tea large enough or a book long enough to suit me," said C. S. Lewis. I wonder if he knows he has his own tea blend. I wonder what he would write if he were sipping it right now. Maybe in the hereafter, C. S. Lewis and Phil Simms can get together and compare the virtues of tea.

Megan D. Willome

Time for Tea

Tea is such a magical product—
perhaps even the eighth
wonder of the world.

H. Rahman, Senior Tea Buyer,
Harrods, Knightsbridge, London

An author friend of mine, who is busy working on a Victorian tea book, recently asked if I could remember a time when the two of us had taken tea together that had a special significance to me. But try as I may, I could not pluck anything outstanding from our Tea Drinking Archives.

How strange, I thought. We must have literally drunk gallons of tea over a thirty-year-plus friendship. Taking tea together was what we did. All the time.

Yes, my friend and I have practically mastered the art of tea-making and tea-drinking down through the years, slowly progressing from matching plastic cups to Royal Albert fine china. We've gone from tea leaves to tea bags and back again. We've switched from sugar to honey, white to black, flavored to plain, back and forth. We've tested it all and made judgment between the correct and the comfortable.

Drinking hot tea, as we do in Australia, is considered a panacea for all ills. Tired? Take a cup of tea! Upset? The only remedy is a hot cup of tea. Visitors? Hospitality dictates the kettle go on as soon as they are seated! At a loss for words? Tea time!

Could it be that we have maintained our friendship because of all those tea times combined? Because each time we shared a cuppa, we were building something very significant . . . a friendship that would last the distance.

Through all the traumas—the taming of toddlers, coping with teens; the pressures of marriage, illness, trials, and tribulations; the challenges of friendship and personality differences—we made it through having tea together. Through moves across town to moves across the world from each other, crisscrossing the Pacific, through interminable phone calls, the advent of grandchildren, the loss of my husband, encroaching old age, and most significant of all, through sharing our faith, we weathered the years, always and forever while sipping hot tea together.

"No," I told my friend, "I cannot think of one significant tea time in all our thirty years of knowing one another that stands out above the others. For each tea time brought a blessing of its own. Each lifting of the teapot between us was yet another step forward, a building block toward something of great value . . . trust, respect, stability, and, above all, unconditional love. The secret ingredient to our lasting friendship has never been the brand of tea or the choice of cup, but rather the time we spent in each other's company."

Lynne Drake

Girls Gone Mild

If your tongue trips over "oolong"
and there's no place for your spoon,
If you end up with your cookie on your
knee, If dainty conversation leaves you
speechless far too soon, You need
some help surviving Ladies' Tea.

Haddyr Leigh

I have two beautiful daughters. They arrived bringing flights of fancy with fairy princesses, dollhouses, and our personal favorite—tea parties. I bought my oldest daughter, Sarah, her first tea set on her third birthday. That same day we filled the tiny plastic teapot with sweet tea, made bologna sandwiches with the crust cut off, and served banana chips with a dollop of peanut butter—Sarah's favorite. Then we sipped tea and chatted about the clouds, the flower garden, and our new puppy. Life couldn't get any better.

When Sarah was five, she was joined by a baby sister. Ashley was barely old enough to hold a teacup when she was invited to join us. And the three of us drank our tea with delight, even though Ashley's table manners at the time left much to be desired.

As the years progressed, so did the tea parties. Bologna sandwiches gave way to cream cheese and cucumber. Sweet tea was replaced by loose-leaf tea we found at various specialty shops. The conversations evolved, as well. We now discussed hairstyles and friendships—important things in the life of "tweenagers."

The girls grew, and Sarah married and moved out. About that time, a teahouse opened in our little town. No more plastic dishes or paper plates for us; we had the real deal. At least once a month, I'd pick Ashley up after high school and we'd head over for tea and scones in the early afternoon. Many times, we were the only ones in the place. Time stood still as Ashley and I talked about her future plans, kids in her class making heartbreaking choices, or whether Sarah's husband was going to be okay while he was stationed in Iraq. Those were deep and precious moments to be treasured.

Ashley, too, grew up and headed off to college. One year during Spring Break, I was blessed to have both girls home at the same time—Sarah from graduate school and Ashley from her second year at the university. This was a rare moment for us, so I headed off to the grocery store to purchase our Easter feast.

🫖 A Liberating Libation

American women led the first rebellion of high taxes on tea from England by refusing to serve tea at their tables.

Later, the Colonists tossed the cargo of three tea ships from England into the Boston Harbor. The British government closed the port, and the American Revolution gained momentum.

When I returned, the girls motioned for me to follow them out to the deck. There was the patio table set with my fine china, complete with linen tablecloth and napkins. The table was laden with cucumber and cream-cheese sandwiches, and completed with banana chips frosted with peanut butter. The girls poured our Blue Lady tea, and we laughed and talked until the sun set. I felt so honored that of all the places my beautiful girls could be on that Spring Break, they chose to be with me. Apparently, I wasn't the only one who valued those treasured moments over tea.

Linda Newton

The World's Worst Tea

The "art of tea" is a
spiritual force for us to share.

Alexandra Stoddard

I was glad I had found a seat in the second-class train compartment, which was as rare as finding snow in the deserts of Rajasthan.

What made it better was that I had found a window seat. Wind, raindrops, feeding monkeys on the way, and buying stuff from hawkers at stations were all part of the "window-seat experience."

The train was delayed, but it didn't matter as I was enjoying the chaotic ambience. It reminded me of the free in-flight entertainment. The only difference was that this was India, and this was real.

Finally, after an hour's delay, the train left Bombay. It was drizzling outside, and everything seemed wet and mossy. Monsoons in India were so much better than the hot summers.

Within thirty minutes, the entire view had changed. Huge construction sites producing tons of dust and noise, helped by India's rapid economic growth, had been replaced by beautiful green fields.

The world outside the train was so incredibly different from the city. There were large areas of green farmland, cows, and barely any humans to be seen. The air smelled fresh, pure, and very cool. I could see power cables running across the fields and a farmer riding his tractor. Of course, the tractors had not yet been able to replace the bullock carts fully. I was still able to see a few cows and bullocks on the fields. The rain got heavier, and raindrops started coming inside the train. Drops of rain splashing over my face and clothes felt nice—more of the "window-seat experience." In the midst of all this, I saw a man coming toward me. He was carrying a basket filled with toys and batteries. He kept shouting in Hindi, "The best quality at the cheapest prices. Toys and batteries for sale." Not many people seemed interested, and they ignored him. I smiled at him and politely shook my head.

After a few minutes, I heard another man shouting. I heard him saying, "The world's worst tea. Nobody can drink it."

I looked and saw a man carrying a big teapot with several disposable plastic glasses. This man seemed like a regular *chai wallah* or tea vendor.

This time, I paid attention. Again, he said the same thing, "The world's worst chai. So horrible that nobody can drink it."

Most people, just like me, stared at him in bewilderment. This man was either a terrible tea vendor or he was plain crazy.

"Such bad tea that one sip, and you will spit it out immediately. The world's worst tea," he continued. Now he had everybody's attention in the train compartment. The world's worst tea started sounding interesting to me. We all have a crazy side that makes some of us jump out of planes and climb mountains; others find ways to fly and explore space. The crazy part of me wanted to find out what the world's worst tea was.

After a couple of seconds, the crazy me took over and signaled him to give me a glass of "the world's worst tea."

Surprisingly, the tea was priced slightly more than normal tea, but it still wasn't very expensive. He smiled and handed me a glass of the tea. It looked normal; I sniffed it a bit before drinking it. It smelled just like normal milk tea.

"Drink it, sir," he said politely.

I drank it. It didn't taste bad at all. I drank more. Still nothing bad happened. In fact, I liked the hint of cardamom and massala. I had been tricked—this wasn't bad at all. It was good. So good that I ended up drinking the entire glass. I looked at him. "You said it was the world's worst tea. It isn't."

"Sir, if I had told you anything else, would you have bought it?"

Yogesh Chabria

3

RELAXING
RENDEZVOUS

porch Tea

In the South, you can't
marry a man until you know how
his mama makes sweet tea.

Author Unknown

My husband and I both grew up in a small Mississippi Delta town where he drank cold, sweet tea at every meal but breakfast. It was really sweet tea, made as only his mother, a true Southerner, could make it. Unlike his family, mine was never big on cold, sweet tea, and my only memory of tea growing up is of hot tea served with a wedge of lemon to ward off the chill of frosty mornings or the beginnings of a sore throat.

When we married and moved away from our little Delta town, my husband missed the tea his momma made. I had not yet learned the secret of making sweet iced tea, and never really thought to ask.

On our trips back to Mississippi, my husband would drink it like it was nectar from above, and I, too, began to acquire a love for its cold, sweet taste. Many a hot afternoon, we would sit out on his momma and daddy's screened porch, embedded in the soft cushions on the white wicker chairs and couches, drinking tea underneath the softly whirring blades of a ceiling fan. The world took on another feel then, and I can still hear the clink of the ice cubes as I lifted the glass to my mouth and remember how the sugar would keep my lips sticky for a while.

Later, on trips to Mississippi when our two girls were old enough to discriminate one taste from another, they soon developed a taste for cold, sweet, Southern tea. But for years I never asked my mother-in-law how she made it. There are so many things that you look forward to when you visit your hometown and family—things that you want to remain special. Maybe I didn't want to turn the tea into something commonplace.

Then, a few years ago, my husband decided to enclose our deck and make it into a screened-in porch. Somewhere around that time, I asked my mother-in-law to tell me the secret of her delicious tea. Why, it was no secret! And it wasn't so difficult to make that I couldn't make it myself. And so one day at home, I made tea. My husband and children were so excited that I soon found myself making pitcher after pitcher of the brew, quickly graduating from quart- to gallon-sized containers for the refrigerator. We gulped it up.

When the porch was finished, we invited our friends over to see it, and we offered them tea. We warned them it was really, really sweet, so sweet that I could sell it to hospitals as glucose. The tea soon had a new name: Glucose Tea. They gulped it up.

I still don't know exactly what it is about sitting on the porch drinking tea that makes it so special. It could be the company. Our girls, now grown, still enjoy it, and we sit, sip, and talk of their plans for the future. Those times pull deeply at the Southerner and mother in me. I feel a sense of continuity. Perhaps our girls will one day have screened-in porches—and their grandmother's tea.

Today, our porch is no longer new, but friends still come over, and we fill their glasses with Southern syrup. It seems they have acquired quite a taste for Glucose Tea. We sit, even on hot nights, out on our screened-in porch where I again hear the clink of ice in the glasses, listen to important things and not-so-important things, hear the sound of a whirring fan, sink into a cushion, lick the sugar off my lips, and smile.

I have learned there is no such thing as commonplace when you have a screened-in porch, family, sweet tea, and company.

Mary Hughes

Margaret's Southern-Style Sweet Tea (aka Glucose Tea)

MAKES A HALF GALLON

6 regular-size tea bags (not family-size)

1 medium pan of water

1 cup sugar

Bring the water to a full boil. Remove from heat.

Add the tea bags, making sure they are immersed in the water. Let the tea bags steep for 15 minutes.

Remove tea bags.

Add sugar; stir well until dissolved.

Pour sugared tea into pitcher.

Let the tea cool before putting in the refrigerator or it may become cloudy.

Mary Hughes

Lessons on a Starlit Night

A cup of tea says to the brain,
"Now rise, and show your strength.
Be eloquent, and deep,
and tender."

Jerome K. Jerome

Steaming and fragrant, a mug of hot tea immediately takes me back to treasured nights spent with my dad. He had a ranch where the edge of the Antelope Valley blends into the Mojave Desert. In the mid-1950s, there were very few other houses, and the night sky was black, except for starlight. On these nights, during the dark phase of the moon, we would bundle up in heavy coats, mittens, mugs of hot tea in hand, and walk out in the night, lit by more stars than any city dweller has ever seen.

Sometimes the fresh-cut alfalfa perfumed the damp night air. Owls, on wide soft wings, would glide by almost silently. Then we would hear a flurry of wings and activity, and know the owl's hunt had been successful.

There, away from the ranch house and shop-building lights, Dad taught me about the constellations. His favorite was Orion, and he noted how the handle of the

Big Dipper pointed to the North Star. He knew names of many more constellations than I could ever remember. Some nights he would review what he had taught me earlier, and some nights were devoted to finding new groupings. His strong arm would slip around my shoulders until he could just tip my chin up to where he was pointing. "There," he would say, "there where the two stars are close and a distance between the next three." I would try so hard to find the formation and remember the name. Some nights, we just sat on the corral fence, sipped our hot tea, and listened to the night sounds of the desert. Occasionally, on these nights, he told old cowboy tales he had heard as a child from cattle drovers.

In spite of Mom's best attempts, Dad never would drink coffee. After I married, I discovered I liked coffee, but will always have a special place in my heart for hot tea. It was the beverage of cold nights, fascinating stories, lessons learned from a most special dad, and spending time with him on those cold, dark desert nights.

Kathleen Kent Hawkinson

Tea Time Is Anytime

When is the right time for tea? It's simple—anytime.

- For you early risers, as you watch the sun come up or grab a few minutes before the frenzy of your day begins, try English breakfast tea.

- Just dropped the kids off at school and have a little break? It's tea time! Reward yourself with a vanilla or chai tea.

- Midmorning munchies are calling your name. Take off the edge with a fruited tea like raspberry, cinnamon, or orange.

- Morning meeting on the agenda? Trade in your cup of joe for a cuppa. Try chamomile if you need to de-stress or peppermint if you're dragging and need a little pick-me-up.

- Ditch your lunchtime soda for a tea. Try Earl Grey so as not to compete with the flavors of your meal. If the weather inside or outside is frightfully warm, have your tea iced.

- Have tea time with your children. Serve them juice in their favorite cups with tiny cookies or mini sandwiches. My kids love peanut butter and jelly cut into teddy-bear shapes and my undivided attention. To extend the fun, cue up the "Mad Hatter's Tea Party" from Disney's *Alice in Wonderland*.

- Stave off an afternoon slump with your trusty cup of green tea for a healthy break and a snack to keep you going. Nosh on an apple, slice of cheese, or almonds, all choices that will keep you energized.

- It's late afternoon and not quite time for dinner. The kids are happily and independently engaged. Slip away for a cup of cinnamon or lemon tea before you have to figure out how to answer the question of, "What's for dinner?"

- Swap your evening glass of wine for a decaf cup of tea and an evening snack. Pair Sleepy Time tea with a cookie, scone, or some berries and whipped cream.

- Enjoy, relax, and remember— anytime is the perfect time for tea.

Tricia Finch

Apple Tea and Crazy Eights

Bread and water can so easily
be toast and tea.

Author Unknown

We'd spent the morning driving through the rocky, hardscrabble beauty of the Bey, a range of Turkey's Taurus Mountains. Erhan, our driver, maneuvered our microbus up and down the February snow-spattered mountain swells and through the streets of terra-cotta-roofed towns like Derekoy and Karamanli. Cows grazed in yards. Men in plastic chairs lined sidewalks, smoking and rubbing prayer beads. Women in billowy pantaloons called *salvar* stooped to sweep porches with handleless brooms, and boys walked fields of just-turned black soil, casting seed from flax bags slung across their shoulders.

Our group was small. Besides Erhan, there was Yesim, our guide, who'd been married a year but had been on the road leading so many tours that she'd spent only sixty days total at home with her husband. Her charges on this trip were me, my son, Adam (then seven and proudly sporting a *Tintin in Istanbul* sweatshirt), Bob and Estheta, a retired couple from Long Island, and Jan and Rose, puckish seventy-something friends from Pennsylvania who'd been globetrotting together for thirty years. They delighted in just about everything and enjoyed pinching Adam's cheeks. We were a well-traveled, glass-half-full lot, and we bonded quickly.

Up in the mountains, the bus door had jammed open, its hydraulic workings kaput, and Erhan had roped it shut against the February chill. This worked for us but violated the tour company's safety code, and it fell to Yesim to get the door fixed.

"Toilet stop," she said, as Erhan eased the bus into a tiny paved lot in front of the Kulcuoglu Restaurant. "We'll be here for fifteen minutes." We weren't fooled. Yesim told Erhan to take the bus to a repair shop in Denizli, the nearest city. It was 11:30. At three that afternoon, Erhan would reappear, door still kaput—he couldn't find an open garage—to collect us.

The restaurant was technically closed. Tourist season began in March, and we were a month early. The owners, an extended family of grandparents, parents, aunts, uncles, and teenagers, were busy readying the place, washing floors and windows, scrubbing toilets, mopping halls and stairs. They weren't prepared for guests, but consistent with the hospitality we'd been shown since landing in Turkey, welcomed us as if we'd been eagerly awaited.

We weren't five minutes inside their door when the first tray of hot apple tea appeared. One of the owners' black-haired daughters came from the kitchen bearing a metal tray of small, clear glasses filled with the steaming, honey-colored beverage. We stood in the hallway sipping the sugared drink, toasting serendipity.

While Yesim stayed downstairs and worked her cell phone, rearranging our itinerary to accommodate what she (and we) knew would be a sizable delay, we followed the father up a worn, wooden staircase to a cavernous dining hall, empty except for stacked tables and chairs and a squat iron stove, quiet and unlit, that sat in the middle of the room. The father pushed a table and six chairs next to the stove, and then fed it from a woodpile by the stairwell. We knew wood was scarce here, and his kindness warmed us before he struck the first match. As the blaze began to hum and crackle, the black-haired daughter mounted the stairs with the second of what would, before the afternoon was out, be a half-dozen trays of apple tea.

The family got on with its cleaning, and we sat, in coats and hats, wondering how to entertain ourselves. Adam, veteran of several global circumnavigations and no stranger to having time to fill in strange places that move at slow paces, rummaged through his *Lion King* backpack and produced the tiny deck of playing cards he'd been given on the British Airways flight we'd taken from Boston to Europe.

Jan and Rose beamed with simultaneous delight when they saw the cards. They clapped and rubbed their palms together. "Gin rummy!" said one or the other or both. They reacted to the lilliputian cards printed with winking, bulb-nosed cartoon airplanes fished from a vinyl Disney bag by a seven-year-old as if a vision of Our Lady of Atlantic City had just descended into the dining hall of the Kulcuoglu

Restaurant. "Gin. We'll teach you," they said, reaching for the deck.

The gin rummy experiment was short-lived, as Adam had the attention span of, well, a seven-year-old, plus an already-established favorite card game: "Let's play Crazy Eights!" I gave Adam a big thumbs-up. Bob and Estheta laughed and told him they loved Crazy Eights, and Jan and Rose pinched his cheeks and told him to deal them in.

For three hours, we huddled at a table by a snapping stove fed with precious wood by a gracious host, playing Crazy Eights with teeny-weeny cards and enjoying sweet swallows of hot apple tea, raising a glass now and then to bus doors going kaput in unexpected places.

Lori Hein

Tea Tasters

● Some master tea tasters at various tea companies throughout the world have the ability to identify between 1,500 and 1,600 different kinds of tea.

● Not only can they identify them, but they can tell you the source of the tea, how it was prepared, even in what season the leaves were picked.

● One famous tea taster can even tell at what elevation the tea leaves are grown.

● After steeping the tea for five minutes, a taster will slurp up a mouthful, swirling it around in his or her mouth, judging the quality, character, and age of the tea before spitting it out. It is the same technique used by wine-tasting experts.

Stop and Smell the Tea Leaves

The spirit of the tea beverage
is one of peace, comfort,
and refinement.

Arthur Gray

My life has often felt like a roller-coaster ride, way too fast, too many curves, and a lot of sharp drops. Eyes tear and the scenery blurs when you're flying through life. Hanging on becomes your primary focus.

Having tea, on the other hand, is more like the carousel. The rhythmic movement of the horses as they go up and down reminds me of the rituals of enjoying a cup of tea. You cannot rush the preparation; most tea blends must brew a minimum of three minutes, an eternity in today's world. Serving tea in a teacup on a tray, with perhaps a cookie or two, allows me time to savor not only the tea, but also everything else that surrounds me. As in the slow turning of the carousel, having tea forces me to sip life rather than gulp it, see the view, pull up a chair, and share a conversation.

My Aunt Carolyn is the first person I recall offering me a cup of tea. The sweetness was the first thing to catch my attention as it lingered on my tongue. I learned there are as many varieties of teas as there are flowers in the garden. In the brewing process, the flavor is released as the hot water comes into contact with each bud and leaf. This slow opening, referred to as the "agony of the leaves," allows the special flavors of each blend of tea to release its magic into every pot. Removing the leaves too early will result in a weak and bland taste. Leaving them too long makes the tea bitter and harsh. Patience is learned as one waits for the proper brewing time, another reminder of why the tea ritual is food for the soul.

Presentation was the next delight. Just like enjoying a pretty dress for a special occasion, there is something about a beautiful, feminine teacup that calls my name.

I fell in love with tea that day and with all things tea-related. Experimenting with different blends of tea and starting a collection of tea accessories became a pastime. Teacups are one of my favorite things to acquire. In the beginning, I chose cups based on a pretty color, popular pattern, or to match my current décor. In the last few years, I became more of a teacup connoisseur and began my Shelley collection. No longer made, and known as one of the most collectable teacups in bone china, Shelley china appears fragile but is amazingly strong, much like many of the women I know. The Shelley dainty teacups have a scalloped edge, almost like a ruffle on a dress. Shelleys are considered the finest in English bone china, and many of the most popular patterns are floral. Chintz is one of my personal favorites.

In researching my new passion, I discovered Shelley was made from China clay, China stone, and calcified beef bone mixed together. Water, when added to the mix, became the slip. Kneading, to reach the required consistency and to remove any air bubbles, transformed the slip to clay. It was then ready for the potter's hand to mold.

Just like the beginnings of the teacup, I've had a less-than-perfect start. The trials I have withstood have not been pleasant, but one by one impurities in my life are being eliminated. I wish I could tell you I'm as translucent as a Shelley teacup, but God is still working on me. As in the agony of the leaves, the hot water I've experienced has released a sweeter aroma, but not without some pain.

There's a reason you don't see drive-through tea rooms or paper teacups. Sharing a cup of tea is a great reminder to stop and smell the tea leaves. The kettle is on, and I've got plenty of teacups if you're interested.

Jo Rae Cash

Sweet Tea and Gratitude

The beauty I see over
tea is thee.

Emilie Barnes,
If Teacups Could Talk

I was sitting in the hospital cafeteria crying like a little girl after hearing that my only son would live the rest of his life as a Type 1 diabetic. He would be required to give himself three to five blood tests and shots every day for the rest of his life.

He was only seven years old. It wasn't fair, so I was feeling very sorry for him and for myself. A kind woman walked by, noticed my tears, and gently touched my shoulder. Although it felt good to connect with someone, I was grateful when she didn't stop. I didn't want to smile and make polite conversation. I wanted to silently curse at a God who would make my child suffer for a lifetime.

When the woman returned with a cup in her hand, I hoped she would just keep going. She did, but not before she placed the full cup in front of me and whispered, "It is chai. It will help."

I thanked her, but I stared at the cup thinking, *I'm not going to drink something with a weird name that a complete stranger put in front of me. I'll wait until she leaves so I don't seem rude.*

The smell coming out of the cup had a wonderful oatmeal-cookie aroma, and it did take my mind off my troubles just for a second. So I picked up the cup and brought it to my nose. Ooh, it was spicy and creamy, and I was reminded of my Grandma Lil's kitchen. The cup was warm in my hands, and the knobby outside of the cup felt natural to me. Before I knew what I was doing, I took a sip and delighted in the feeling. It tasted like comfort. I turned to look for the woman who had given me the tea, but she was gone.

My son stayed in the hospital three days while they educated all of us about what food he could eat, how to take blood for tests, and inject insulin. On the third day, we were in the administration office waiting to sign paperwork for his discharge when my son noticed a coffee kiosk across the hall that sold pastries. He desperately wanted a muffin, and it broke my heart that he couldn't have one. I scanned the menu for something he could have, but there were no sugar-free treats. Then I noticed on the tea menu that they did have sugar-free chai, so I ordered one for both of us.

I remembered the kind woman who had said, "It will help." And I watched my son's face to see if it worked as well for him as it did for me. *He loved it!*

"Shane," I said, "there is an entire universe of things out there that you have not tried. Let's think of this as the first."

Suddenly, it occurred to me that God wasn't cursing my son with suffering. He was giving both of us a reason to seek out things we normally wouldn't have tried. Although the shots and tests would become as much a part of our everyday lives as toothbrushing or showering, the search for new treats would offer us many gifts. It would offer stories like the one my husband told of buying chai on a train in India served in little clay cups. One would drink the super sweet tea and discard the cup alongside tracks that were red with years of cracked cups. It would offer us trips to new cities to try sugar-free chocolate from companies like Harry London. And it gave us a reason to take up exercise in new ways, such as our monthly "noodle" (slow bicycle ride in the country) and scootering in local parks.

I can't say it's always been easy, but Shane is sixteen now and has lived more than half his life as an insulin-dependent diabetic. He has tried ethnic foods of more than fifteen countries, started a *Get Better Newsletter* for young people who have been diagnosed with diabetes, and has competed in several walks for charities.

What could have been a tragedy for our entire family was turned into a triumph by a stranger in a hospital with a cup of sweet tea.

Dawn Howard

High Tea in Singapore

A man travels the world over
in search of what he needs, and
returns home to find it.

George Moore

"Ligh Tea? Singapore?" I gasped. My mind's eye split the world-globe in half as I pictured the small island that stretched lazily along the equator. Hot and humid.

From halfway across the United States, our son, Dave, was on the phone. "How would the two of you like to stay in Singapore for three weeks or so? I'll be working there for several months. Debi will be joining me. Mom, you and Debi can go to High Tea in Singapore!" Dave's enthusiasm extended from their house to ours.

In a moment's time, my husband accepted the invitation. "Why not?" he said. "Our suitcase handles are always warm."

So we quickly prepared to spend time overseas with this dear young couple. They were perfect for each other. The only thing missing in their lives was a longed-for child.

Darkness had fallen when, after seventeen hours of

travel, we arrived at the Singapore airport. The date and time on the calendar registered midnight a whole day later. Because we had crossed the International Date Line, we had lost a day, and . . . a lot of sleep.

"Seems like an awfully long way to go for tea," I teased our son, Dave, when he greeted us.

Once settled in our fourteenth-floor apartment, starry-eyed, we watched the city lights sparkle at night. During the day, we were at eye level with the tall, beautiful buildings of Singapore. One gaze at the pool below coaxed us to use the "lift" and drop down to poolside. Afternoon tea and scones, served at "hawf-past three," delighted us, drawing us from our lounge chairs into the cool of the apartment building's lobby. Life was good. We checked off our long list of things to do. The days sailed by.

Saving the best for last, Debi and I reserved an afternoon for High Tea at the Raffles Hotel. Dressed in our fanciest clothes, we stepped from our cab in front of the posh hotel. A nattily dressed doorman opened the door for us, and we entered a realm of beauty and history.

A white-gloved waiter, a folded towel over his arm, motioned for us. His formal white trousers and long-sleeved jacket with gold buttons seemed right out of a romance novel or fairy tale. "Please be seated, ladies," he said. He then informed us of the tea, finger sandwiches, pastries, and tropical fruit available to us. He smiled broadly. With a professional bow he promised he would return to see to our needs.

Our cozy table for two, draped with a long white tablecloth, held an exquisite bone-china teapot and delicate cups. Mine was designed with delicate yellow and purple painted pansies—one of my favorite flowers. Debi's cup, painted with vibrant red roses, suited her charm and vivaciousness.

A large table filled with endless goodies—exquisitely sumptuous, elegant, and luxurious—coaxed us to help ourselves. Between nibbles of the delicious food and sips of flavorful tea, I gazed around this lovely room. I noticed Debi giggling to herself.

"What?" I asked.

Debi grinned at me. "Well, I've heard they started using the name High Tea after some famished person spoke up around four o'clock one afternoon saying, 'It's high time we had some tea!'" We laughed and motioned for our waiter to return with more tea. "Tell us more about tea," we pleaded. He did not disappoint us.

"According to Chinese legend, thousands of years ago, leaves from a wild tree blew into a pot of boiling water a man was tending. Intrigued by the pleasant scent, he drank some. That was the beginning of tea drinking. Of course, the British colonized Singapore, and they were habitual tea drinkers. It is a daily occurrence on our island." He bowed and wished us a pleasant "awfternoon." "Please continue with your tea and delectables," he added.

After our third trip to the constantly replenished table, our mood lifted higher with every sugar-filled bite. We became like two schoolgirls trying to stifle giggles in a library while the stern librarian peered at them over her glasses.

"English Breakfast tea is my favorite, even in the afternoon at High Tea," said Debi, taking another long, flavorful swallow.

Just then, we noticed a young family lingering at the door before entering and strolling past our table. The adorable cherub-like infant slept soundly on its mother's shoulder. Suddenly, my beautiful Debi's eyes filled with tears.

Sadly, I glanced at the tea leaves in the bottom of my cup. Some people say you can read your future in them, but I only saw tiny bits of leaves in a half-empty cup, like prayers waiting to be answered.

Within a few days, our time had come to leave Singapore. Dave and Debi hopped a short flight to the Island of Bali for the weekend.

Shortly after arriving home in the Midwest, our phone rang. Dave and Debi were both on the line. "You won't believe this," they exclaimed. "We got a call while we were in Bali to come home to California to be interviewed. We have been chosen to be the adoptive parents of a baby boy."

Now tears of joy flowed all around. Our prayers were answered. Our cup was full!

Marilyn Jaskulke

A Spot for a Spot

In the 1880s in England, tea shops became the rage thanks to the manager of one of the Associated Bread Company (ABC) bake shops.

He routinely invited his friends and a few customers into the back room to enjoy a cup of tea. The custom caught on, and within a few years ABC tea shops were everywhere, welcoming weary shoppers to sit awhile and enjoy a good brew with all the accoutrements that a good bake shop can provide.

One of the most famous of the tea-shop chains in the United Kingdom was Lyons. Two hundred fifty Lyons tea shops bestowed grace and glamour on the tea drinkers of England. Many boasted orchestras, potted palm trees, and an atmosphere fit for royalty. Waitresses served trays filled with steaming pots of tea, mini-sandwiches, and luscious cakes.

Today, tea rooms still buzz with lively conversation, old family recipes, and luscious cups of glorious tea.

A Peppermint-Tea Miracle

Ecstasy is a glass full of tea and
a piece of sugar in the mouth.

Aleksandr Pushkin

I lay on the couch, hunched into a ball, hands on my nauseated stomach. Influenza had hit me hard, and I was unable to keep up with my sixteen-month-old, Tyler. When he wasn't racing around, he was crawling all over me. My poor body ached. I yearned to be left alone so I could crawl into bed.

Fortunately, my husband, Gordy, came home to help so I was able to escape to bed without worrying about Tyler. But the next morning when I awoke to my toddler's crying, Gordy had already left for work, and I still felt horrible.

As I lay there, I turned to God. "Lord, I just can't make it today without you. You will have to take charge of my home today—please help me keep Tyler safe!"

After Tyler and I had been up for a few hours, I felt a bit better. It was a beautiful, sunny day. My son begged to go "Owside! Owside!" I finally relented and put him in his stroller, hoping the fresh air would revive me.

We headed up the hill, but after a few blocks I turned around, lacking energy to go any farther. I must have been a pitiful sight—crouched over the stroller as it supported my weight. On our way past one neighbor's house, she cracked open her door and leaned out.

"Are you okay? You don't look well."

Feeling dizzy, I looked at Helen, gave a weak smile, and replied, "Oh, it's just a flu bug. I thought I was getting over it, but I'll be okay. Thanks for asking."

"I've heard that flu is going around—hope you feel better soon."

As I continued down the hill, my thoughts wandered back to Helen and her husband, who had recently moved to our little town to retire. My heart reached out to them. They seemed lonely and bored.

Only three years before, Gordy and I had been the newcomers. Thankfully, we had immediately begun attending an intimate local church and had also made new friends by getting involved in community activities. As the stroller bumped and jerked on our gravel driveway, I steadied it with one hand and felt my forehead with the other. Hot. My brain felt foggy. Thank goodness we were home.

I lugged Tyler—who seemed twenty pounds heavier—up the stairs, and thought again of Helen and Bill. Was there a way I could reach out to them, to make them feel more welcome?

After I had collapsed on the couch, Tyler and I watched television and read stories for a while. My stomach cramped and ached terribly. What in the world would help?

Suddenly, I remembered that I'd heard something, somewhere, about how peppermint tea soothed the stomach. I knew I didn't have any in the cupboard, so I decided to go to the store. As I grabbed my purse, I realized I felt too ill to drive anywhere. *Oh, well,* I thought, *I don't know if the tea will actually help anyway.* As I stood there, halfway to the door, keys in hand, the doorbell rang.

Who could that be? I thought. I sure wasn't up for entertaining. Hesitantly, I opened the door to find Bill, Helen's husband.

"Helen wanted me to give you this," he said, as he handed me a small, colorful bag, "because you're not feeling well." I smiled, then opened the bag.

"Oh!" For a moment, I was speechless. Inside were some balloons, cookies, and, of all things, peppermint tea! I stood staring at it in amazement. "Thank you! You may not believe this, but only moments ago I wanted some of this exact kind of tea. I just felt too sick to go to the store to buy some. God must have used you two to answer my prayers today. Give Helen my thanks, will you?"

After good-byes, I put on the teakettle, and then blew up a few balloons. Tyler was soon occupied and giggling. I

🫖 It's in the Bag

Tea bags were accidentally discovered in 1904 when a tea merchant sent samples of loose tea in small, silken bags. His customers assumed they were to immerse the bag and all into the boiling water.

The silk bags were too fine, so gauze bags were used, then finally paper tea bags were invented.

In the early 1960s, tea bags made up less than 3 percent of the British tea market, but by 2006, tea sold in tea bags represented 96 percent of the British market.

watched him as I relaxed in the recliner, sipping my tea. Within minutes, it soothed my stomach as nothing else had. We even shared the freshly baked cookies.

In the months that followed, as Tyler and I would be out strolling, Helen would often see us through her window and urge us to come inside for a visit. Cradling warm drinks in our hands, we sometimes talked of the graciousness of God. And we often reminisced about the day he prompted her to send me a simple, yet perfectly timed, gift of peppermint tea.

Laurie Winslow Sargent

Everyday Tea

It has been well said that tea is
suggestive of a thousand wants, from
which spring the decencies and
luxuries of civilization.

Agnes Repplier

I learned to drink tea at a very early age. My Scots-Irish grandmother owned a small neighborhood bakery, and for the first five years of my life, my mother and I spent our weekday mornings in the working area of that establishment. I learned early on that I was to stay out of the way of those who worked at the high tables, and that the sales area of the bakery remained forbidden territory.

Many were the times that I crept to the doorway and peeked into the room where glass cases held the delectable treats my grandmother created. Cakes and pies, bread and rolls, coffee cakes and cookies lined the shelves. I watched with interest as a young Czech girl served customers. More than once, a firm hand circled my arm, pulled me none too gently away from the doorway, and scolded me on the way to the long picnic table that ran across one end of the workroom. The pale green oilcloth cover served as background to white cups and saucers that waited to be filled with the strong, hot tea brewed in a plain brown teapot. "You can only make good tea in a plain brown pot," Grandma remarked on many occasions.

Grandma served the tea, but when she came to mine, she poured only half a cup. Then she added a spoonful of sugar and filled my cup to the top with milk. "English tea for you," she'd say. Never would our tea be savored all by itself. Grandma always had a plate of something fresh from the oven. Cinnamon rolls, or sliced coffee cakes, or a muffin. To this day, I like a little bit of something sweet to go with my tea. The scent of yeast and spices surrounded us as we sipped the tea. In wintertime, we enjoyed the waves of warmth from the ovens, and in summer we put up with the combined heat of the outside temperature and those never-empty ovens while we had our everyday tea.

I lifted my cup with both hands and sipped at my "English tea," listening to Mother and my uncle chat. I nibbled on one of the goodies Grandma passed to me, and I knew only contentment. I liked sitting at the long table during the tea break, swinging my legs, waiting for the time when they would all return to work and I could plan my next peek out front.

One Saturday afternoon after the baking had been done, Grandma came to our apartment. She was dressed in a tailored suit and wore a hat that had big pink roses on it. She carried white gloves and a handbag. She wasn't the grandma I knew, the one who wore a Mother Hubbard apron over her plain cotton dress every day. "We're going to Marshall Field's today to have our tea," she told me. I looked at my mother to see what she thought about this new situation. She smiled and repeated the oft-used phrase of all mothers in the early 1940s, "Be a good girl."

Grandma and I rode the elevated train to downtown Chicago. The conductor called out the stops, and finally, Grandma tugged at my hand. We stepped out onto a wooden platform where we were greeted by a symphony of traffic sounds. Pigeons strutted nearby, pecking at peanuts tossed on the platform. I was fascinated by the soft gray birds and would have stayed to watch them, but Grandma whisked me through a set of double doors that led into the famed Marshall Fields store. We walked straight into the china department. Glorious china, crystal, silver, and linens were displayed on dining-room tables. But there was no tea here.

My little-girl legs worked hard to keep up with Grandma as she led the way to the elevators. "Seven please," Grandma said to the operator, and up we went. The doors opened, and we stepped into the magnificent Walnut Room. Dark paneled walls, soft carpet, and pot-ted palms surrounded us. A hostess led us to a small table draped with a snowy linen cloth. Other ladies with suits, hats, and gloves sat at similar tables. I felt a tickle in my tummy for I knew now that this would not be an everyday tea. Something special awaited us in this elegant dining room.

Grandma spoke softly to a uniformed waitress, then set-tled into her chair and graced me with a warm smile. Her face looked softer than it did at the bakery where she spent so many hours. Even at my young age, I knew my grandma worked hard.

Soon, the waitress returned to our table. She placed a small plate, fork and spoon, a china teacup and saucer in front of each of us. A linen napkin finished the setting. Ladies nearby sipped tea and nibbled at tiny sandwiches and small iced cakes. Oh, if only we were to have the same. The tickle in my tummy started up again, and I wiggled on my chair in anticipation.

Sure enough, the waitress brought a lovely flowered teapot and two plates. One held dainty open-faced sandwiches, and pastel-iced cakes filled the second one. I waited for Grandma to tell the waitress that good tea could only be made in a plain brown teapot, but she never said a word. Instead, she poured my half cup of tea, and added sugar and milk. Then she placed a sandwich and a cake on my plate. I watched her lay the napkin on her lap, and I followed her example. Just as I was to take my first bite, piano music interrupted the sound of spoons on saucers and ladies conversing. Soon, several tall, slender women strolled through the vast Tea Room, stopping momentarily at an occasional table. "It's a fashion show," Grandma whispered to me. The models wore the kind of dresses and hats we saw only in the movies. They glided and pirouetted, faces looking like they were set in stone, but a strange thing happened as they approached us. Each one who stopped at our table looked right at me and smiled. One even winked. Now the tickle in my tummy felt like butterflies chasing each other.

All too soon the fashion show ended, and we'd had our fill of the tea, sandwiches, and cakes. We rode the train home where I related the events of the day to my mother and father.

I had tea with Grandma at the picnic table in the bakery many, many times, but she never took me to the Walnut Room again. Long after my grandma was gone, I returned to Marshall Fields for tea on my own, and sometimes I'd look across the table and see my grandma in her rose-covered hat smiling at me. She taught me the difference between everyday tea and special tea, that a little something sweet came with both kinds of tea—but sweetest of all were the memories my grandma created. I feel her near each time I pour my everyday tea from my plain brown pot.

Nancy Julien Kopp

My Mother's Tea Set

Life should be savored:
sipped like a cup of tea.

Author Unknown

I mposing in the foyer of my Honolulu apartment, the wooden crate stood five feet high and two feet square around. I had been waiting for this package for months, and I felt a surge of excitement as I struggled with shears and a screwdriver, slicing through the girdle of metal bands and prying open the reluctant boards. Inside, I knew, was a precious family heirloom—my mother's Wedgwood tea set.

In Stoke-on-Trent, England, where I grew up, the tea set was a part of daily home life at Denstone, our red-and-white brick bungalow on Birkholme Drive. My mother would have her "nice cuppa" every morning, and on weekends, my dad delivered the floral cup and saucer—just a little milk, no sugar, thank you—to her in bed. This ritual seemed quite grand to my six-year-old imagination, and I decided then that the lady of the house should always be served tea in bed.

Breakfast wasn't the only occasion for tea. Each evening when my dad came home from work, there would be a cup and saucer alongside his dinner kippers. The teacup also ventured out of doors regularly as, with each cup consumed, my mother emptied its soggy tea-leaf contents onto the ground outside our kitchen door as fertilizer for the healthy red rosebush that climbed up the wall almost to the roof.

A wedding present from my mother's parents, the tea set took on a new importance for me many years after we had immigrated to America and settled in Williamsport, Pennsylvania. I learned that just before World War II broke out in Europe, my mother, a teenager, had taken a job with one of the many manufacturers of bone china in the five boroughs that make up Stoke-on-Trent—also known in England as The Potteries. In a windowless room filled with pottery dust, girls worked in pairs. As one partner meticulously cut out the design with specialized scissors, the other (my mother) affixed it to the teacup or saucer before sending the item to the kiln. The girls were paid by the number of pieces they could finish.

Now the tea set had a significance far beyond its utility. It gave me a secret glimpse into my mother's life as a "Potteries' girl." The tea set continued in service until we moved to California during my high-school years, when it was put aside in favor of the more casual and utilitarian mug. My mother still took her morning tea, but not in her bone-china teacup, which languished behind cupboard doors in ignoble exile. When my parents retired, they moved to Nevada, furnishing their new home with, among other things, a stately oak china cabinet. Finally, the tea set was on display, brought out and used on

special occasions, a delightful reminder of travels, traditions, and new beginnings. There it remained until now,
passed down to the eldest daughter.

As I gently held one of the delicate cup-and-saucer pairs
that had made its way across two oceans and a continent
to become a part of my home as it had my mother's, I
noticed a faded spot on the handle where a portion of the
gold decorative line had been rubbed off by the repeated
nesting of a forefinger. All of a sudden, I felt bereft, missing her, but she was not one for sentimentality. There was
only one thing to do now, I decided. I would make myself
a nice cup of tea and retire to the bedroom.

Jennifer Crites

Drink to Your Health!

Both black and green teas are high in antioxidants called flavonoids, a type of chemical found in all plants that helps to protect them from harm.

Antioxidants help prevent damage to cells from free radicals that are byproducts of normal metabolism. Tea provides about 22 percent of the total intake of flavonoids in the U.S. diet. (Vegetables provide 26 percent, and fruits provide 28 percent.) Studies suggest that the flavonoids in tea are more potent than vitamin E. One-hundred-fifty milligrams of flavonoids, the amount found in a cup of brewed tea, is enough to have an immediate antioxidant effect.

Although both black and green tea come from the same plant, the oxidation of black tea during processing creates different flavonoids from those found in green tea, which does not go through the oxidation process. Both black and green teas should be consumed on a regular basis to ensure intake of the full range of tea's different flavonoids.

Brewing tea for five minutes extracts about 80 percent of the antioxidant capacity of the flavonoids. Instant tea and bottled teas are much lower in antioxidant capacity than fresh-brewed tea from either loose leaves or tea bags. Therefore, to get the most health benefit from tea, brew it yourself.

A Courtship Served with Tea

If man has no tea in him,
he is incapable of understanding
truth and beauty.

Japanese Proverb

I t began with an e-mail asking me out for tea. The message came from my neighbor, Chris. I had met him in the parking lot the day before, where we stood for quite a while chatting. He piqued my interest with his e-mail invitation, since he had no way of knowing that I was an avid tea drinker.

The night of our first date, our "tea date," we went to a local tea and coffee shop downtown. Chris and I sat on tall wooden chairs around a high table facing the expansive front window. The sidewalks glistened from a fresh rainfall, tiny white lights sparkled in the leafless trees lining the street, and storefronts displayed colorful items for the coming spring.

I sipped my jasmine tea, and Chris drank his Earl Grey. The two of us watched evening strollers window shop while talking about our childhoods and our reasons for moving to the area. He captivated me with his sense of humor and warmth.

Normally a quiet person, I found myself opening up to him and enthusiastically discussing a wide range of subjects. We talked through the night, and I was continually amazed at how much we had in common. It was as if Chris and I had known each other far longer than just a few short hours.

By the end of that first date, I knew I had met a very special man.

That night and the weeks that followed were bittersweet, though. During our date, Chris broke the news that he had already accepted a college teaching job in Texas, and would be moving in a few months for the start of the new school year.

"I'll understand if you don't want to see me again," he said solemnly, "but I hope that you do."

I had finally met a man with whom I felt totally alive, and he was moving across the country for a new job. My rational mind told me I was crazy to keep dating him, but another part of me knew that the connection I had found with Chris was rare and advised me not to lose him. So I continued to date him and lived each day enjoying his company, all the while trying not to think of August when he would be leaving.

Then, on a Tuesday evening a month later, Chris was at my apartment having dinner. We had just finished eating when he handed me a tin canister and said, "I thought you might like this."

It was a tin of Wuyi Oolong tea. The label said that silver-tipped leaf tea was "one of the world's most rare and highly prized teas." I opened the canister and inhaled the peachy aroma. When I peered inside, something shiny among the dark tea leaves caught my eye.

"Oh, look, the company put a little prize in . . ." my voice trailed off as I tried to comprehend what I was seeing. I glanced up at Chris, and he grinned at me. I shook the tin slightly and uncovered the object fully. Realization finally sank in . . . an engagement ring! Gingerly, I plucked the ring from the leaves and put it on. It sparkled on my finger, brightening the entire apartment.

Chris's face turned earnest. "I'm not going to Texas, Laura. Now that I've found you, I'm not leaving." Then, on one knee, he proposed.

My answer was, "Yes, most definitely, yes." The rest of the night was a blur—telling relatives, talking about our future, and staring at my ring. I do remember clearly that the tea filled me with a warm glow.

Chris and I were married a few months later. Through the years, our quiet time together has mellowed into a weekend morning tea ritual. The first one to wake goes downstairs and prepares the morning tea. The pot is warmed, the scones heated, and our tea tray is arranged with the feast.

Upstairs once again, my husband and I enjoy a leisurely hour or so reading, sipping tea, eating scones, and talking. It is a chance for us to relax and enjoy each other's company.

We are not always successful in our attempt to block off time for our morning ritual, but sharing those peaceful moments over tea has become an important part of our lives.

Unknowingly, my husband began a theme in our relationship when he first asked me out for tea, a theme of tea infused with romance. It is a combination that both he and I are content to keep happily brewing long into the future.

Laura Schroll

Tea Time for Tommy and Me

Tea quenches tears and thirst.

Jeanine Larmoth and Charlotte Turgeon

G rowing up, a breakfast staple for us was a cup of green tea with milk and sugar, and cinnamon toast. Mom would line up the four cups on the kitchen counter, and the tea would steep while we got dressed for school. Every morning, for as far back as I can remember, tea was an important part of our morning ritual. I like to think it was also the liquid that blended, for a moment, sibling love.

When my brother, Tommy, was a teenager, I was the gawky kid sister he never wanted around—especially when his friends were over. But there were times when he could be nice.

At the age of about fifteen, Mom let him pursue his hobby of raising homing pigeons. One particular pigeon named King was his pride and joy.

Being in a good mood one day, he took King out of the wire cage in the backyard and let me hold him. One frenzied flap of the wings, and I panicked and let go. Old King went flying into the wild blue yonder, and Tommy flew off the handle, yelling at me.

I was about nine at the time and desperately wanted to do something to make it up to him. I had a plan. I filled the teakettle with water and set out four of Mom's best coffee cups, one for Tommy and each of his friends. I placed a tea bag in each cup and filled them to the rim with the steaming water.

I found some vanilla wafers in the pantry and placed them on a fancy saucer. I added the milk and sugar to the tea, as Mom did each morning, and then wondered how I'd transport my tea-time treat outside to where the boys were flying remote-controlled model airplanes.

I looked around the house and found my almost-perfect, makeshift serving tray. It was the top piece of a toy piano. Its weird, oblong shape, which narrowed in the middle, looked goofy, but it did manage to hold the cups and cookies nicely, allowing me to navigate my piano-top tray out the door and to the edge of the yard where Tommy and his friends were hanging out.

When they saw me coming, they looked at me as if I was a teapot short of a whistle. The friends ran off, leaving Tommy and me with four cups of hot tea to drink in the middle of a hot summer's afternoon.

Tommy did drink the tea offered, and so did I. It was one of those very rare bonding moments between a brother and sister who never had all that much in common.

I have no idea where my brother is these days. He left home years ago, never again to be part of our family. But there are mornings when I'm sitting at the kitchen table, enjoying my cup of tea while savoring a precious memory of tea time with Tommy.

Kathleen Gade

A Secret Weapon

- Some research suggests that tea may help keep your teeth and bones healthy while boosting your immune system at the same time.

- Cavities are caused by bacteria, sugar, and acid. Tea drinking helps reduce cavities because it contains fluoride in its leaves. Fluoride makes tooth enamel stronger and resistant to acids.

- Tea inhibits the growth of bacteria in the mouth and also keeps it from sticking to the surfaces of the teeth. Tea also decreases the activity of the enzyme responsible for breaking down starch into sugar in the mouth.

Tea for Two

Tea for two and two for tea.
Just me for you, and you for me alone.

Irving Caesar

Flying along at 34,000 feet, I could faintly hear the hum of the engines, and I snuggled down in my seat. Memories of the past weekend swirled in my head.

My husband and I had traveled to Silverdale, Washington, to see our daughter, Jennifer, and her family. This was an exciting event as she had been living in Japan for three years and had only visited us twice.

It was cold, being the middle of February, and the wind off Puget Sound blew in a storm that turned the sky a slate gray.

"Hey, Mom, let's go into town and get away by ourselves for awhile," my daughter suggested. "Dad and Ed can watch the kids; it'll do them good to bond for awhile."

Never one to miss a shopping expedition with my daughter, especially one I hadn't seen in years, I was ecstatic.

"Ready when you are," I yelled out from the guest bedroom. "But it looks like it's really going to pour. Are you sure we shouldn't stay home?"

"Are you kidding? Mom, it rains up here a lot. We just keep on going."

"Okay," I said, grabbing my new down coat. "Let's go."

We hopped into her car and took off.

"Mom, there is this really cool store I want to show you. Do you like tea?"

"Sure. I've started drinking it more often lately, especially with all the health benefits they've discovered."

"Well, you're gonna love this place. Wait 'til you see it."

We walked into this little, out-of-the-way store hidden in the back of the strip mall. Floor-to-ceiling shelves lined the walls with huge glass-barrel jars full of tea: Jasmine Pearl, Rooibos, Hibiscus, Jade Oolong, Chrysanthemum Blossom, White Peony, Earl Grey, and Darjeeling—the list went on and on. I never knew there were so many kinds of tea. The smell that wafted by my nose was heavenly. You could buy any quantity you wanted, and the matronly little lady behind the counter was very animated and helpful.

"Anything you would like to smell? You can get an idea of the flavor that way. Any questions, I'm right here." And with that she was off to dust the shelves.

I sniffed over twenty jars of tea, and they all smelled delicious. Some were fruity, some spicy, and some smelled like flowers. I ended up buying about ten two-ounce bags of tea. Of course, I had to buy a tea ball and a simmer pot, and a few new teacups to round out the set.

"Jennifer, I love that place," I said on the way home.

"I go in there a lot, now that I've learned to drink so much tea from being in Japan. Let's go home and try some."

"Aren't we going anywhere else?" I asked, disappointed. I didn't want our time alone to end.

"Not unless you really want to. I just wanted to share that tea shop with you."

I thought maybe Jennifer had been teasing me about carrying on, no matter what the weather, and we headed home.

The sky had turned even darker, and the first raindrops hit the car with huge "kerplunks" on the window.

The guys had taken the kids down to the marina, so we were alone. First, Jennifer lit the fireplace and brought out a tiny, carved cherrywood table that she put in front of the fire. She placed two cups on the table, scurried into the kitchen, and turned on the burner under her teapot.

I could barely hear it whistle as the wind howled outside. The rain was coming down so hard it lashed the house furiously.

We sat on the living-room floor in front of the fire, shoes off, an afghan over our legs. She poured our tea and smiled as the storm raged on.

"You planned all this, didn't you?" I asked.

"Well, the rain was someone else's idea, but being here alone with you—the crackling fire, the hot tea—it's been my fantasy for a long time, Mom."

We had our own little tea party that day, long overdue, and although it was cold and wet outside, my heart was warm and glowing.

A "thunk" brought me back. As the landing gear came down, I realized it wouldn't be long before we were home again. I patted my carryon bag full of my precious teas. That day would live in my memory forever, but meanwhile, I had my teas to comfort me until we were together again.

Sallie A. Rodman

Taking Time

World-peace conferences
would run more smoothly if a nice cup
of tea, or indeed, a samovar, were
available at the proper time.

Marlene Dietrich

What on earth was she doing? Frau Amtmann, my German landlady, stood in the kitchen flinging what looked like spoonfuls of dirt into an elegant teapot. I summoned up my elementary German. *"Was machen Sie?"* (What are you doing?)

"Making tea," she replied.

I wasn't a tea drinker. In fact, I had never in my life tasted tea. But this couldn't be right.

"Oh, no," I protested. "Tea only comes in bags!"

Frau Amtmann laughed, looking at me with a mixture of astonishment and pity. She said nothing, but I could see she was sizing me up. What she saw was a twenty-one-year-old American woman who clearly needed to be taken under her wing. I didn't know it at the time, but my education in the fine art of living had just begun. And Lesson Number One was the liquid amber of a well-made tea.

The fact that our two life paths had crossed was entirely coincidence. My husband and I, newly married, had come to Munich in the summer of 1970 with a modest fellowship for his study abroad. In an ancient VW Beetle, we crisscrossed the city, viewing one dreary, overpriced lodging after another. Finally, a clerk at the foreign student office gave us a tip. She told us of a woman who liked having "interesting" people renting rooms in her house. It was outside the city, she said, in a small village south of Munich. Hoping that being American made us sufficiently exotic, we set off immediately.

The address led us past fields and forest to a fairy-tale villa nestled in a large, bright garden. And, yes, we could rent the tiny two-room suite upstairs. Even better, Frau Amtmann, the lady of the house, was looking for a housekeeper, so I could easily earn enough to pay our rent. The christening cup of tea marked the beginning of my household education. Frau Amtmann, always in a dress, her graying hair swept into a perfect French twist, instructed me in everything from darning socks and shining shoes to waxing parquet floors. In the kitchen, where I sometimes helped, I witnessed wonder upon wonder—puddings made without instant powder, cakes prepared without a mix, tender deep green lettuce replacing the pale crunch of iceberg. And from the town bakery, a revelation—rich, dark breads with real crust, and crispy rolls that opened with a snap. With housework filling only the morning hours, the days flowed slowly by, and more often than not, wended their way toward afternoon tea.

In my memory of those days, it is always winter. Frau Amtmann and I take a walk, rambling through snowy, pine-sweet woods as a blue sky dazzles overhead. Back at the house, with snow-packed boots deposited in the hall, we busy ourselves preparing tea. The whistling kettle steams the windows. A still-warm *Apfelkuchen* (apple cake) gets a final sprinkle of powdered sugar. I carry a generous wooden tray, piled with our treasures, to the round table in the living room. As I settle into my usual armchair, Frau Amtmann serves. The tea is strong. The flavor—even softened with sugar and milk—stays bold.

And then we talk. In my maturing but still stumbling German, we talk about America. About the war in Vietnam. About civil rights and Black Power. We talk about German music. Bavarian humor. And World War II—in 1970, not so very far in the past. We discuss family. Childrearing. Public schools. Catholic schools. Boarding schools. We agree. We disagree. We talk until the room glows briefly in the twilight, then slips into shadow. Frau Amtmann lights a single, tall candle, and the pot, kept warm by a flickering tea light, keeps delivering.

Ever since my Munich year, I have rarely missed an afternoon cup of tea, even if it had to be brewed at my desk in an office mug or sipped from a Thermos at a chilly soccer game. Why am I so obstinately faithful to this daily ritual? Because for me, tea carries something deeper than flavor. Always, just beyond the mellow taste, lingers a hint of that special year when life slowed down to a stroll, and I had the chance to look at a new world with new eyes.

And so I have come to understand Frau Amtmann's lesson. Taking tea is about taking time. Time to prepare food with care. Time to talk. To think. To pause. To enjoy. I don't always manage to take that time—the world, it seems, turns far too quickly on its axis—but with every sip of tea, I do appreciate the gentle reminder.

Eleanor Rosellini

"I bet his owner is an instant coffee drinker—
no *tea drinker* would own a dog like *that!*"

Steeped in History

- Tea is second only to water as the most popular beverage in the entire world.

- Chinese literature gives credit to Emperor Shen Nung, known as the Divine Healer, for inventing tea more than 5,000 years ago. He boiled his water before drinking it, and one day leaves from a tree fell into the pot, resulting in a fragrant and delicious tea.

- Tea arrived in Europe in 1560 thanks to a Portuguese Jesuit priest, Father Jasper de Cruz.

Afternoon Tea

The afternoon glow is brightening
the bamboos, the fountains are bubbling
with delight, the soughing of the pines
is heard in our kettle. Let us linger in the
beautiful foolishness of things.

Okakura Kakuzo

W hen my sister and her family relocated to Scottsdale, Arizona, thirteen years ago, I knew our lifelong closeness was about to be tested. She and I had become accustomed to living near each other in New Jersey, our homes ten minutes apart. To complete the beauty of our situation, her youngest daughter, then four, and mine at age nine, enjoyed playing together.

Since the kind of contact we had taken for granted all our lives could not continue, we vowed to make every effort to create special and meaningful experiences for the four of us during visits. At the end of December each year, when both girls are off from school, my daughter and I travel to Scottsdale, where my sister commandeers us through a slew of activities on her new turf. We enjoy the hearty mountain hikes, marvel at the strange cacti, explore old frontier towns, and bounce around gleefully on desert Jeep tours. All that robust outdoor adventure leaves us ready for what has become the highlight of every Arizona visit: Afternoon Tea at the elegant Phoenician Hotel.

This is not simply tea, the drink; it is Tea, the Experience. It involves gliding through the elegant hotel lobby filled with marble columns and impressive artwork; being escorted to a luxurious couch in a light, expansive parlor overlooking a deck and pool as a piano player fills the room with gentle tunes; and imbibing an assortment of freshly brewed teas poured for us into delicate china cups. We have learned that Afternoon Tea was originally designed for the British aristocracy to enjoy a delightful midday break of snacks and conversation—with tea. This is not to be confused with High Tea, which sounds sophisticated, but is actually what the lower classes called their main meal. For our annual Afternoon Tea, the four of us are upper class, and we attempt to behave accordingly!

With this goal in mind, we spend the morning of our outing primping enthusiastically. This is part of our ritual, and we embrace its silliness. For this brief period of time, we are four giggly roommates in a dorm, trying on one another's clothes and critiquing one another's hair and makeup. When we arrive at the hotel, beautifully coiffed and attired, we are ready to embrace the main part of the ritual. Seated on our couch, ankles crossed demurely, we study the gold printed menu. We pay careful attention to our server's explanation of the history of the china being used and of the designs on the porcelain.

As if it is the most important decision we will ever make—and on that special day, it is—we discuss the various tea flavors and select the ones to order. We have tried blackberry currant—our favorite, with its tangy taste—as well as vanilla and jasmine. We settle on three new ones to try and await the food. Tiny little sandwiches will be served first, then scones, and finally, an assortment of desserts.

When our selections are gently placed before us on the beautifully carved coffee table, we find ourselves eating and drinking in a manner totally unlike our usual. We reach for the little watercress with egg and cucumber with dill cream-cheese sandwiches with care; we taste the scones with utmost refinement of manners, delicately licking our lips and nodding appreciatively at one another as we sample the Devonshire cream topping; we clasp our hands in silent joy as the array of tempting pastries is presented. We *ooh* and *ahh* over the tiny custards topped with berries, the mini chocolate-mousse pies, the lemon-meringue tarts. We watch in awe as the fragrant tea is poured from an exotic teapot painted with colorful butterflies and birds—a teapot with its own history as part of a partially lost British set—and then we lift our cups to drink with our little pinkies extending outward. We taste and savor and discuss the various tea flavors. We dab at our pursed lips daintily with the soft cloth napkins.

Finally, our stomachs full, we use the time to truly talk. In this peaceful setting, free of arguments and interruptions, we can spend hours sipping, laughing, reminiscing. The sweetness of our tea-talks, like the sweetness of the fruit-filled pastries, mingles with the warmth of the tea coursing down our throats. We recognize that the comforting and flavorful teas—combined with the tea atmosphere—have come to represent all that we share.

On this one outing a year, the four of us are transformed. We are no longer middle-aged mothers or teenagers, with the problems and pressures each faces. For that afternoon, we are four little girls playing Let's Pretend and Dress Up. We are four rich and poised ladies with not a care in the world. We are four women cementing our bond, reaffirming our sisterhood. Two sisters, two daughters. Escaping the mundane concerns of everyday life, escaping the fact that we no longer live in close proximity, escaping the passage of time and the intrusion of unpleasantness in life. Through indulging in the fragile magic of Afternoon Tea together, we allow ourselves to savor, with the tea, the strength and beauty of our bond, which we renew with each visit.

Nothing can replace what my sister and I once had, when our homes were in the same vicinity and our lives more directly intertwined. But we have dedicated ourselves to remaining close by sharing distinctive experiences in order to make the most of the time that we do have. So when we say good-bye at the Phoenix airport each year before my daughter and I return to New Jersey, we hug and cry and thank each other for everything. But we also make a promise that seals the bond of our sisterhood—Afternoon Tea again next year.

Ruth Rotkowitz

Monday-Night Tea

Nobody can teach you
how to make the perfect cup of tea.
It just happens over time.
Wearing cashmere helps,
of course.

Jill Dupleix

"Mom!" my exasperated eight-year-old pouted glumly. "That's your '*no* look.' All the other kids go see the Cookie Lady every day. Can't I go, please?"

This same request had punctuated every afternoon since shortly after we'd moved to this new area of town. A lady who gave away cookies to small children made me wonder if we had made the right move. But surely, I reasoned silently, all of these children's parents must know this person if they allowed daily visits.

Sighing reluctantly, I looked at the five eager faces outside our screen door and made up my mind. I grabbed my daughter's hand, bowing playfully, "Okay, Princess. I am your royal subject. Lead me to the Cookie Lady." Giggling in delight, the children pulled and led me (like a pied piper in reverse, I thought) hopping and skipping down the street past the other homes that were similar in size to ours.

When I realized we were heading around the bend, I stopped in my tracks, suddenly shy. Our family had walked the neighborhood and noticed the half-dozen imposing, column-fronted homes on the bend. We had not yet seen or met any of their owners, and several of the neighbors were in awe of the financial power these homes represented. It was almost as if the bend contained an imaginary boundary.

"Come on," the children urged, pulling me along to a beautiful, red-brick two-story. Beating me to the door, I was awed that the children saw no difference in the two neighborhoods as they rang the doorbell. Beautiful multi-toned chimes harmonized a welcome while I mentally compared it to the "ding-dong" of our own doorbell.

I was completely disarmed by the tall, elegant lady who answered the door. She gave each of the children an obviously homemade sugar cookie centered with a pecan half. Business done, the six little ones lined up on her porch and munched happily, allowing Magdalene Veenstra to introduce herself as "Grandma V" and correctly guess that I was Cheri's mom. I accepted a cookie as well and listened to her charming story of how she once offered store-bought cookies, which were instantly rejected by several children who announced they would return when she felt better and made the good cookies again. Five minutes later, I left, bemused at her warm invitation to join her for a cup of tea the following Monday night.

A junior-high home-economics class was my only preparation of protocol for that first Monday-night tea, and I wore a skirt to honor her generation and her genteel nature. When she opened the door, my aproned hostess did not need to tell me she had been baking. I followed her to the kitchen with an anticipation that never dimmed over the following fifteen years of our Monday-night tea.

Instantly comfortable, she directed me to a seat at the yellow-topped table, and I watched the ritual—as I came to think of her tea preparations—while drooling (inwardly only, I hoped) over the freshly baked delicacies for two that she'd placed in the precise center of the delicate pink English china plates.

I was pleasantly surprised as she sat and bowed her head in prayer. Realizing that this longed-for grand-mother figure also shared my faith instantly drew our hearts closer.

From that Monday on, recipes filled our conversa-tions—not only recipes for her famous cookies, but recipes for living, for walking-the-faith, for loving our families, and eventually even for dying.

Each cup of tea opened a chapter of a living history book with tales of war, the Depression, numerous presi-dents, life on several continents, and the invention of radio, airplanes, automobiles, and television.

Over the years, her eyes failed, and she asked me to read to her. Her hearing was also limited, so I sat on a cushioned footstool at her feet. She had ceased most cook-ing and had shocked the motor-vehicle department by voluntarily giving up her license with a simple, "It's time."

Distressed by her inactivity, I once thought I could encourage her with some gentle chiding to follow one of her favorite pieces of advice, "Use it or lose it." She leaned forward so that we were practically nose-to-nose. I gave her my full attention as she looked me straight in the eye, paused for effect, and said, "You ever been ninety-three?"

We laughed the rest of the night over her remark and my shocked reaction. As usual, though, I was on the way home when I realized the lesson amid the humor. I cannot lead where I have not gone. There is a time to walk before (the next generation) and a time to walk behind (the last generation), but always—always—the time is right to walk beside . . . especially if you offer a cup of tea.

Delores Liesner

Sensuali-Tea

If the world seems cold to you,
kindle fires to warm it.

Lucy Larcom

H issing and boiling, there it sits. A sassy little thing, plump and full-bellied, Dumbo-eared. My well-used, well-worn, copper teakettle.

See how it's tarnished from age? Just look at all the scratches. Oh, and did you notice the dent? I dropped the poor thing on its snout one time. Even so, all was forgiven, and we're still a faithful twosome. Day after day, year after year, we find comfort in each other.

Whether tea is sipped in bed between April-crisp sheets, among the leafy arbors in your tea-castle garden, from the veranda glider at dusk on a summer's day, or in the big armchair while wearing your warmest socks, there is something singular about a soul-soothing cup of the hot beverage.

Tea seduces your senses.

The practiced routine of brewing has a tactile rhythm all its own that brings a relaxation of mind and spirit. Fresh water from a cold tap. Warm patina on a copper kettle. Friendly flames from a gas range. Soon, you hear a full-throated gurgling. You pour a bit of boiling water into your ceramic teapot, swill it around, empty it out. Add brittle tea leaves. Flood with burbling water. Cover to simmer and steep.

Fragrant tendrils of steam seep out of the spout to tempt, tickle, and tease. Oolong, Ceylon, or sage. Jasmine, pekoe, or pearl. Mind-mellowing concoctions conjure mysterious peoples and exotic settings. Take a moment to inhale ancient times and lands. Allow yourself to hold the comfort of the ages in your own hand.

Which is it to be today? The last teacup from Grandma's set of bone china with its matching saucer? Or perhaps the chipped mug that reads: *Forget the din of the world*?

You pour to the brim, add a sugar cube, and stir. Puff away the steam. Take a test sip. And another. *Ahhhhhh.* The flavorful drink slips down your throat and seeps through your limbs until, finally, it melts your middle.

Tea warms the heart, eases the body, piques the senses. It's a symbol. One of those little blessings that reminds us to enjoy life . . . sip by tiny sip.

Carol McAdoo Rehme

More Chicken Soup?

We would love to hear your reactions to the stories in this book. Please let us know what your favorite stories were and how they affected you.

Many of the stories and poems you have read in this book were submitted by readers like you who had read earlier Chicken Soup for the Soul books. We publish at least five or six Chicken Soup for the Soul books every year. We invite you to contribute a story to one of these future volumes.

Stories may be up to 1,200 words and must uplift or inspire. You may submit an original piece, something you have read, or your favorite quotation on your refrigerator door.

To obtain a copy of our submission guidelines and a listing of upcoming Chicken Soup books, please write, fax, or check our web sites. Please send your submissions to:

Chicken Soup for the Soul
P.O. Box 30880
Santa Barbara, CA 93130
Fax: 805-563-2945
Website: www.chickensoup.com

Just send a copy of your stories and other pieces to the above address. We will be sure that both you and the author are credited for your submission.

For information about speaking engagements, other books, audiotapes, workshops, and training programs, please contact any of our authors directly.

Supporting Others

All over the world, millions of innocent people are caught up in intolerable situations. But they are not today's victims; they are tomorrow's heroes, who have the power to transform their own communities.

The publisher and authors of *Chicken Soup for the Chocolate Lover's Soul, Tea Lover's Soul, Coffee Lover's Soul,* and *Wine Lover's Soul* are pleased to donate five cents from the sale of each of these four books, up to $1 million per book to Mercy Corps, an organization that exists to alleviate suffering, poverty, and oppression by helping people build secure, productive, and just communities.

Mercy Corps works amid disasters, conflicts, chronic poverty, and instability to unleash the potential of people who can win against nearly impossible odds. Since 1979, Mercy Corps has provided $1.3 billion in assistance to people in 100 nations. Supported by headquarters offices in North America, Europe, and Asia, the agency's unified global programs employ 3,400 staff worldwide and reach nearly 14.4 million people in more than 35 countries.

Mercy Corps has learned that communities recovering from war or social upheaval must be the agents of their own transformation for change to endure. It's only when communities set their own agendas, raise their own resources, and implement programs themselves, that their first successes result in the renewed hope, confidence, and skills to continue development.

Your purchase of this title has helped support Mercy Corps, but if you would like to do more or would like more information about the great work they do, please contact them.

Mercy Corps
3015 SW 1st Avenue
Portland, OR 97201
Phone: 800-292-3355
Website: www.mercycorps.org

Who Is Jack Canfield?

Jack Canfield is the cocreator and editor of the Chicken Soup for the Soul series, which *Time* magazine has called "the publishing phenomenon of the decade." Jack is also the coauthor of eight other bestselling books, including *The Success Principles: How to Get from Where You Are to Where You Want to Be, Dare to Win, The Aladdin Factor, You've Got to Read This Book,* and *The Power of Focus: How to Hit Your Business, Personal and Financial Targets with Absolute Certainty.*

Jack offers an online coaching program based on The Success Principles and offers a seven-day Breakthrough to Success seminar every summer, which attracts 400 people from fifteen countries around the world. Jack is the CEO of Chicken Soup for the Soul Enterprises and the Canfield Training Group in Santa Barbara, California, and founder of the Foundation for Self-Esteem in Culver City, California. He has conducted intensive personal and professional development seminars on the principles of success for over 900,000 people in twenty-one countries around the world. He has spoken to hundreds of thousands of others at numerous conferences and conventions and has been seen by millions of viewers on national television shows such as *The Today Show, Fox and Friends, Inside Edition, Hard Copy, CNN's Talk Back Live, 20/20, Eye to Eye,* and the *NBC Nightly News* and the *CBS Evening News.*

Jack is the recipient of many awards and honors, including three honorary doctorates and a Guinness World Records Certificate for having seven Chicken Soup for the Soul books appearing on the *New York Times* bestseller list on May 24, 1998. To write to Jack or for inquiries about Jack as a speaker, his coaching programs, or his seminars, use the following contact information:

Jack Canfield, The Canfield Companies
P.O. Box 30880 • Santa Barbara, CA 93130
Phone: 805-563-2935 • Fax: 805-563-2945
E-mail: info@jackcanfield.com • Website: www.jackcanfield.com

Who Is Mark Victor Hansen?

In the area of human potential, no one is more respected than Mark Victor Hansen. For more than thirty years, Mark has focused solely on helping people from all walks of life reshape their personal vision of what's possible. His powerful messages of possibility, opportunity, and action have created powerful change in thousands of organizations and millions of individuals worldwide.

He is a sought-after keynote speaker, best-selling author, and marketing maven. Mark is a prolific writer with many best-selling books, such as *The One Minute Millionaire, The Power of Focus, The Aladdin Factor,* and *Dare to Win,* in addition to the Chicken Soup for the Soul series. Mark is the founder of the MEGA Seminar Series. MEGA Book Marketing University and Building Your MEGA Speaking Empire are annual conferences where Mark coaches and teaches new and aspiring authors, speakers, and experts on building lucrative publishing and speaking careers. He has appeared on television (*Oprah,* CNN, and *The Today Show*), in print (*Time, U.S. News & World Report, USA Today, New York Times,* and *Entrepreneur*), and on countless radio interviews.

As a philanthropist and humanitarian, Mark works tirelessly for organizations such as Habitat for Humanity, American Red Cross, March of Dimes, Childhelp USA, and many others. He is the recipient of numerous awards that honor his entrepreneurial spirit, philanthropic heart, and business acumen. He is a lifetime member of the Horatio Alger Association of Distinguished Americans, an organization that honored Mark with the prestigious Horatio Alger Award for his extraordinary life achievements. Mark Victor Hansen is an enthusiastic crusader of what's possible and is driven to make the world a better place.

Mark Victor Hansen & Associates, Inc.
P.O. Box 7665 • Newport Beach, CA 92658
Phone: 949-764-2640 • Fax: 949-722-6912
Website: www.markvictorhansen.com

Who Is Patricia Lorenz?

Patricia Lorenz is the coauthor of *Chicken Soup for the Chocolate Lover's Soul*, and *Chicken Soup for the Dieter's Soul Daily Inspirations*, and she is one of the most frequent contributing writers to the Chicken Soup for the Soul series, with stories in over thirty editions.

Patricia is the author of *Life's Too Short to Fold Your Underwear, Grab the Extinguisher My Birthday Cake's on Fire, Great American Outhouse Stories, True Pilot Stories, A Hug a Day for Single Parents*, and *Stuff That Matters for Single Parents*. She has had over 400 articles published in numerous magazines and newspapers, is an award-winning newspaper columnist, and a contributing writer to seventeen Daily Guideposts books and over sixty anthologies.

As a professional speaker Patricia has entertained hundreds of groups throughout the United States with her art-of-living speeches, with topics including Humor for the Health of It, Follow Your Dreams While You're Still Awake, The Five Things We Need to Be Happy, and Learning to Love Your Struggles. She is also a sought-after speaker for women's retreats and writing conferences.

Patricia lives in Largo, Florida, where she moved after twenty-four years in Milwaukee, Wisconsin. She is the mother of four grown children and the proud grandmother of eight.

To contact Patricia about speaking engagements, visit her on the Web at www.PatriciaLorenz.com, or e-mail patricialorenz@juno.com.

contributors

The stories in this book are original pieces or taken from previously published sources, such as books, magazines, and newspapers. If you would like to contact any of the contributors for information about their writing or would like to invite them to speak in your community, look for their contact information included in their biography.

Shirley J. Babcock lives in a log house in northern Wisconsin working on peace, justice, and environmental issues; sorting through unfinished writings of experiences started as a teenager; and relaxing daily with a cup of bush tea. She began writing seriously after attending the School of the Arts in Rhinelander.

Aaron Bacall's work has appeared in most national publications, several cartoon collections, and has been used for advertising, greeting cards, wall calendars and several corporate promotional books. Three of his cartoons are featured in the permanent collection at the Harvard Business School's Baker Library. Aaron can be reached at abacall@msn.com.

Pearl Blanchette, an ardent tea lover, has lived in the United States since 1949. She began writing in 1985. She won first place in a University of Wisconsin writing contest, and was published in *Nostalgia Magazine, Good Old Days, Mature American,* and other senior publications. She was a reporter for Community Newspapers.

Isabel Bearman Bucher's work ranges from research to stories of the heart. With Robert, her husband of twenty-eight years, she travels the world on home exchanges. She enjoys four children, five grandchildren, and one great-grandson. Her book, *Nonno's Monkey: An Italian-American Memoir,* is set in the 1940s and told from an oft-confused, six-year-old point of view. Visit Isabel at www.oneitaliana.com.

Jean Campion, the author of *Minta Forever,* a historical novel, taught writing at Fort Lewis College in Durango, Colorado, for fifteen years. She has written for and edited several publications. She has been married to her high-school sweetheart for over forty years, and they have three grown children.

Joel A. Carillet is a freelance writer and photographer. His work, which has appeared in venues such as the *Christian Science Monitor,* seeks to shed light on humanity, both our own and that of others. More of his work can be found at http://jcarillet.gather.com.

Jo Rae Cash is a freelance writer and inspirational speaker. She has a devotion in the *One Year Life Verse Devotional* (September 2007, Tyndale House Publishers) and is a contributor to the Chicken Soup for the Soul series. In addition to writing, Jo Rae enjoys tennis, gardening, and tea. She lives in Simpsonville, South Carolina, and can be reached at t4me@bellsouth.net.

Yogesh Chabria, besides being a "chai addict," helps people create wealth through his company GSIFS.com. He is a published writer and motivational speaker, and loves making people laugh. He is interested in learning the art of "keeping his room less messy." All potential teachers can e-mail him through www.GSIFS.com.

Jennifer Crites is a freelance writer/photographer whose work covers a wide range of subjects from travel to contemporary lifestyles and science. Her words and images have appeared in *Islands*, the *New Yorker*, *Travel+Leisure*, Fodor's travel guides, and other publications, and she is co-author and photographer of a nature book, *Sharks and Rays of Hawaii*. Visit her website at www.jennifercritesphotography.com.

Lola Di Giulio De Maci loves writing for children. Her inspiration comes from her now-grown children and the many children she has taught over the years. She is a contributor to Chicken Soup for the Soul books, as well as being an inspirational speaker. She writes in a sunny, sky-blue loft with a panoramic view of the San Bernardino mountains. E-mail her at LDeMaci@aol.com.

Lynne Drake is a pastor, author and poet, international speaker, and founder of God's Heart Ministry. She lives in New South Wales, Australia, but travels widely throughout Africa, the United States, and India. Her writings appear in magazines and online devotionals. She may be reached at lynnedrake@bigpond.com. Her website is www.Gods-heart.com.

Janet Perez Eckles is an inspirational speaker, writer, and author of *Trials of Today, Treasures for Tomorrow: Overcoming Adversities in Life*. Visit Janet at www.janetperez.com.

Sherrie Eldridge, an author and speaker, specializes in the subject of adoption. Visit her website, www.adoptionjewels.org, for a wealth of adoption resources. Sherrie often enjoys tea with her youngest granddaughters, Olivia and Megan, in a little tea room she created for them. Of course, everyone wears old-fashioned hats and glittery shawls.

Susan Engebrecht grew up surrounded by story spinners. Thus, following in her ancestral footsteps to have her stories and poems published in literary books, newspapers, and inspirational magazines, as well as on radio broadcasts, came naturally. She claims her greatest gifts to the universe are two sons and five grandchildren.

Tricia Finch lives in Venice, Florida with her husband Jeff, son Nicholas, two dogs and two cats. Formerly a youth librarian, she is now a stay-at-home mom and freelance writer. She enjoys reading, scrapbooking, and having fun with her family. Tricia's work has appeared in local and national publications and was featured in *Chicken Soup for the Dieter's Soul*. Visit her at http://home.comcast.net/~tdfinch.

Kathleen Gade (pen name) is a newspaper columnist who shares her sentimental musings on family life. Her writings have been featured in various anthologies, including, *The Golden Formula* and *Finding the Joy in Alzheimer's*. Kathy and her husband Bill are recent empty nesters who are finding that the honeymoon isn't over—it's only just begun! You may reach Kathy by e-mail at kathywhirity@yahoo.com.

Cathy C. Hall is a humor columnist for the Gwinnett edition of *Our Town Magazine*, and also writes an online column called "Stirred Crazy" at SanityCentral.com. Cathy is a guest columnist for the *Atlanta Journal-Constitution*, and will someday finish her juvenile fiction . . . right after she writes one more Chicken Soup for the Soul story!

Linda Marie Harris began her writing career at the age of ten when she wrote a story entitled "Change of Life." Linda's mother promptly told her to *change* the title! Since then Linda has written stories, personal vignettes, a children's book, and poetry. She is married with two grown children, two dogs, three cats, a goldfish, and two koi.

Jonny Hawkins has been cartooning professionally since 1986. His work has appeared in over 370 publications, such as *Reader's Digest, Forbes, Boy's Life* and *Woman's World*. His books, including *The Awesome Book of Healthy Humor*, and his *Cartoon-A-Day* calendars are available everywhere.

Kathleen Kent Hawkinson, a native Californian, is a professional organist and pianist. Also a published photographer and writer, she has many writing styles and subjects, but her favorites are poetry, devotionals, and children's books. Kathie is married and has one adult daughter. She can be reached via e-mail at muzikmakin@aol.com.

Lori Hein (www.LoriHein.com) is the author of *Ribbons of Highway: A Mother-Child Journey Across America* and a contributor to several Chicken Soup for the Soul books. Lori's writing and photography have appeared in publications nationwide and online. She publishes a world travel blog at www.RibbonsofHighway.blogspot.com.

Ilene Herman is a proud mom, grandma, and great-grandma who holds degrees in Speech and Hearing Therapy and Applied History. She was a verse writer for *American Greetings*, and has authored local history books and a monthly column for a San Leandro, California, publication. Ilene also enjoys work as a museum docent and trainer.

Dawn Howard is a full-time mom and part-time writer who writes content for websites and trade journals. This is her second contribution to the Chicken Soup for the Soul series.

Mary Hughes writes for her church website, has been a guest columnist for her local paper, and has her own monthly subscription-based newsletter, *Christian Potpourri*, which will also be available online soon. On most warm days you can find her on her back porch sipping tea, and watching and listening for inspiration.

Sydney Salter Husseman lives in Utah with her husband, two daughters, two cats, and two oversized dogs. She has written stories for *Appleseeds, Children's Playmate, Faces, Hopscotch, Story Friends, Wee Ones Magazine,* and Blooming Tree Press's *Summer*

Shorts anthology. She loves reading, writing, traveling, and baking delicious treats for her tea parties.

Robbie Iobst, blessed wife of John and proud mom of Noah, is a freelance writer and speaker. She lives in Centennial, Colorado, and is a member of Words for the Journey Christian Writer's Guild. In her spare time, Robbie loves to scrapbook, read, and enjoy a spot of tea.

Marilyn Jaskulke is a freelance writer. Originally from Minnesota, she and her husband have retired to southern California, where writing has become a new adventure. Recent articles have been published in *Mature Living* and *Chicken Soup for the Golfer's Soul*. E-mail her at mar68jask@cox.net.

Nancy Julien Kopp has published stories, articles, essays, children's stories, and poetry in magazines, newspapers, e-zines, and anthologies, including *Chicken Soup for the Father and Daughter Soul, Chicken Soup for the Sister Soul II,* and *Chicken Soup for the Dieter's Soul*. She is a former teacher who still enjoys teaching through the written word.

Charlotte A. Lanham first learned to drink hot tea in Sydney, Australia. She loved it so much that she moved back to Texas and opened her very own Victorian tea room. Now retired, she is a freelance writer, speaker, and frequent contributor to *Chicken Soup for the Soul* books. E-mail her at charlotte.lanham@sbcglobal.net.

Delores Liesner of Racine, Wisconsin, is sharing the contagious joy of God's humor in her life through print, including several Chicken Soup for the Soul volumes, radio, and television. You can reach Delores and find her book, *Eating with Dave—A Healthy Response to a Cancer Diagnosis*, on www.eatingwithdave.com.

Evelina M. Mabini fell in love with writing at the age of twelve when her father brought her to a writers' meeting. Her work has appeared in a number of publications, including *Catholic Digest* and *Care Notes*. She was a pediatrician for more than twenty-five years and is now retired and a proud grandmother of twin toddlers and two pre-schoolers.

Anita Machek's work appears in the *Beauregard Daily News,* the *Rosepine Register, Hometown Shopper,* and the *Jasper Peddler*. Pelican Publishing recently accepted her submission to the Louisiana in Words project, an anthology of short pieces relating one minute in Louisiana.

Julia Miller has lived in Arizona and Connecticut and is currently a hospice chaplain in West Virginia, but the little New Jersey town where she grew up is still dear to her heart. Julia enjoys afternoon tea with friends and has a grown son, a daughter-in-law, and two grandsons who keep her supplied with tea and stories.

Amanda Monette resides in northern Alberta. She is a wife and stay-at-home mom of two wonderful young children. Giving piano lessons also brings her great joy. Writing has always been an interest of hers as she has written numerous short stories, many based on true happenings in her life.

Linda Newton is a Pastoral Counselor on staff at Sierra Pines Church in Oakhurst, California. The mother of three grown children, she enjoys speaking, writing, and tea parties with her daughters. Visit her online at www.lindanewtonspeaks.com.

Dorri Olds, a native New Yorker, earned a BFA in 1985 and has been a graphic designer ever since. In 1994, she started her Manhattan-based business, www.DorriOlds.com. Her short stories have been published in two Chicken Soup for the Soul books, in *New Woman* magazine, and in the book, *At Grandmother's Table*.

Janice Olson writes poetry, non-fiction, and children's and adult fiction. She is the author of devotionals and a Texas blog, and coauthor of a how-to book, along with contributing to several e-zines on the Internet. Janice is an active member of American Christian Fiction Writers and the Society of Children's Writers and Illustrators. You may contact her at janice@jkolson.com.

Carol McAdoo Rehme directs a nonprofit agency, Vintage Voices, Inc. She is a prolific writer, editor, and coauthor of numerous gift books. Her latest project, *Chicken Soup for the Empty Nester's Soul*, will be released in 2008. Self-pampering helps maintain her sanity—and vanilla bean tea is just the ticket! Contact her at carol@rehme.com.

Bruce Robinson is an award-winning, internationally published cartoonist whose work has appeared in numerous consumer and trade periodicals including the *National Enquirer*, the *Saturday Evening Post, Woman's World, The Sun, First, Highlights for Children*, and more. He is also author of the cartoon book, *Good Medicine*. You can reach Bruce by e-mail at cartoonsbybrucerobinson@hotmail.com.

Sallie A. Rodman has written for many Chicken Soup for the Soul anthologies, various magazines, and the *O.C. Register*. She and her husband plan to make more trips to Washington State to visit her daughter and family. She also intends to revisit the tea shop to try more exotic blends. E-mail her at sa.rodman@verizon.net.

Eleanor Rosellini is an environmental activist and the author of the *Hidden Treasure Mysteries*, a detective series for 9- to 12-year-olds in which a brother-and-sister detective team solve long-forgotten mysteries from the past. She and her husband, a professor of German literature, have two grown children. Visit www.hiddentreasuremysteries.com.

Ruth Rotkowitz is a freelance writer who has written for a variety of publications, including *Chicken Soup for the Sister's Soul 2, Hopscotch*, and *Expecting*. She is currently at work on a novel and a screenplay. She can be reached at mideb@aol.com.

Laurie Winslow Sargent is the author of *Delight in Your Child's Design* and *The Power of Parent-Child Play*, and has contributed articles/stories to: *Chicken Soup for the Christian Soul II, Roar! A Christian Family Guide to the Chronicles of Narnia, Kisses of Sunshine for Women, The Write Start: Practical Advice for Successful Writing*, and *Christian Parenting Answers: Before Birth to Five Years Old*. Visit Laurie at www.ParentChildPlay.com.

Laura Schroll is a freelance writer living on Long Island, New York. Her essays and articles have appeared in various publications, including *Chicken Soup for the Dieter's*

Soul, Tea: A Magazine, the *Tea Time Gazette,* and *A Cup of Comfort for Mothers-to-Be.*

Priscilla Gertrude Simmons is a freelance writer, retired church secretary, and cottage worker who resides in Ephrata, Pennsylvania, with Barry, her husband of forty years. Pricilla has three children, one son-in-law, and three grandchildren.

Scott Sutton, an English as a Second Language teacher, has backpacked in more than thirty countries. He taught in Loa refugee camps in Thailand, was a reporter in Hong Kong, and studied literature in Russia. He is published in several genres: Christian, political, and travel. His first novel, *Desert Redemption,* was released in 2005.

B. J. Taylor is an award-winning author whose work has appeared in *Guideposts,* many Chicken Soup for the Soul books, and numerous magazines and newspapers. She has a wonderful husband, four children, and two adorable grandsons. Visit B. J. at www.clik.to/bjtaylor.

Eileen Valinoti is a freelance writer whose work has appeared in popular magazines such as *Parents, Glamour,* and *Health,* and in *Chicken Soup for the Working Woman's Soul.*

Samantha Ducloux Waltz is an award-winning freelance writer in Portland, Oregon. Her personal essays are her favorite way to sort out her always interesting, often chaotic world, and can be enjoyed in a number of current anthologies and the *Christian Science Monitor.*

Janie Dempsey Watts' essays have been published in *Chicken Soup for the Horse Lover's Soul* (1st and 2nd editions), *Guideposts, Georgia Backroads,* and at www.boomer womenspeak.com. She also wrote a novel, *Moon Over Taylor's Ridge,* and is at work on a second. Janie lives in Woodstation, Georgia, and has been drinking tea since she was old enough to hold a china cup.

Elizabeth Wells' work has appeared in national newspapers and magazines, including *Life in the Times, Highlights, Crayola Kids, Liguorian,* and *U.S. Catholic.* She is a regular contributor to *From House to Home,* has written several books on travel and cooking, and is busy on new book projects. You can reach Elizabeth at elwells@cox.net.

Cheryl E. Williams is a retired freelance writer residing in western Pennsylvania. She enjoys family activities, attending writers' functions, gardening, and raising pet parakeets.

Megan D. Willome is a regular contributor to the *Wacoan* magazine, a monthly lifestyle publication. Her poem "Labyrinth" will be published this fall in the *Inspirit* literary journal. She cannot begin writing without a pot of tea and Garrison Keillor's *The Writer's Almanac* for the day.

Enjoy the entire series!

Code #6306 • $14.95

Code #6241 • $14.95

Code #6292 • $14.95

Code #6314 • $14.95

Also Available

Chicken Soup African American Soul
Chicken Soup African American Woman's Soul
Chicken Soup Breast Cancer Survivor's Soul
Chicken Soup Bride's Soul
Chicken Soup Caregiver's Soul
Chicken Soup Cat Lover's Soul
Chicken Soup Christian Family Soul
Chicken Soup College Soul
Chicken Soup Couple's Soul
Chicken Soup Dieter's Soul
Chicken Soup Dog Lover's Soul
Chicken Soup Entrepreneur's Soul
Chicken Soup Expectant Mother's Soul
Chicken Soup Father's Soul
Chicken Soup Fisherman's Soul
Chicken Soup Girlfriend's Soul
Chicken Soup Golden Soul
Chicken Soup Golfer's Soul, Vol. I, II
Chicken Soup Horse Lover's Soul, Vol. I, II
Chicken Soup Inspire a Woman's Soul
Chicken Soup Kid's Soul, Vol. I, II
Chicken Soup Mother's Soul, Vol. I, II
Chicken Soup Parent's Soul
Chicken Soup Pet Lover's Soul
Chicken Soup Preteen Soul, Vol. I, II
Chicken Soup Scrapbooker's Soul
Chicken Soup Sister's Soul, Vol. I, II
Chicken Soup Shopper's Soul
Chicken Soup Soul, Vol. I-VI
Chicken Soup at Work
Chicken Soup Sports Fan's Soul
Chicken Soup Teenage Soul, Vol. I-IV
Chicken Soup Woman's Soul, Vol. I, II